Treasures

Practice Book O

W9-AZC-591

**Macmillan
McGraw-Hill**

B

The *McGraw·Hill* Companies

**Macmillan
McGraw-Hill**

Published by Macmillan/McGraw-Hill, of McGraw-Hill Education, a division of The McGraw-Hill Companies, Inc.,
Two Penn Plaza, New York, New York 10121.

Printed in the United States of America

5 6 7 8 9 10 045 09 08 07

Contents

Unit I • Relationships

School Days
David's New Friends

Short *a* and *i* 1
Vocabulary 2
Comprehension: Character and Setting Chart 3
Comprehension: Character and Setting 4
Fluency 5
Vocabulary Strategy: Alphabetical Order 6
Short *a* and *i;* Words with *-s, -es* 7
Text Feature: Photos and Captions 8

Making Friends
Mr. Putter & Tabby Pour the Tea

Short *o, e, u* 9
Vocabulary 10
Comprehension: Story Map 11
Comprehension: Plot 12
Fluency 13
Vocabulary Strategy: Base Words and Inflected Verbs 14
Short *o, e, u;* Inflectional Endings *-ed, -ing* 15
Text Feature: List 16

Firefighters at Work
Time For Kids: *Fighting the Fire*

Short and Long *a* 17
Vocabulary 18
Comprehension: Main Idea and Details Web 19
Comprehension: Main Idea and Details 20
Vocabulary Strategy: Word Families *-ell, -eat* 21
Study Skills: Using Parts of a Book 22
Fluency 23
Short and Long *a;* Suffixes *-er, -est* 24

Being Yourself
Meet Rosina

Short and Long *i* 25
Vocabulary 26
Comprehension: Main Idea and Details Web 27
Comprehension: Main Idea and Details 28
Fluency 29
Vocabulary Strategy: New Meanings for Known Words 30
Short and Long *i;* Inflectional Endings *-ed, -ing* 31
Literary Elements: Rhyme and Rhythmic Patterns 32

Coming to America
My Name Is Yoon

Short and Long *o* 33
Vocabulary 34
Comprehension: Predictions Chart 35
Comprehension: Make and Confirm Predictions 36
Fluency 37
Vocabulary Strategy: Inflected Verbs 38
Short and Long *o;* Inflectional Endings *-s, -es* 39
Text Feature: Graphs 40
Review: Vocabulary 41
Review: Vocabulary 42

Unit 2 • Growth and Change

Plants Alive!
The Tiny Seed

Short and Long *u* 43
Vocabulary 44
Comprehension: Conclusion Chart 45
Comprehension: Draw Conclusions 46
Fluency 47
Vocabulary Strategy: Use Context Clues 48
Short and Long *u;* Words with -*er*, -*est* 49
Text Feature: Diagrams and Labels 50

Animal Rescue
A Harbor Seal Pup
Grows Up

Consonant Blends: *sl*, *dr*, *sk*, *sp*, *st* 51
Vocabulary 52
Comprehension: Sequence Chart 53
Comprehension: Sequence 54
Fluency 55
Vocabulary Strategy: Antonyms 56
Consonant Blends; Compound Words 57
Literary Element: Similes 58

A Hospital Visit
Time For Kids: *A Trip to*
the Emergency Room

Long *a*: *ay*, *ai* 59
Vocabulary 60
Comprehension: Sequence Chart 61
Comprehension: Sequence 62
Vocabulary Strategy: Homophones 63
Study Skills: Using the Library 64
Fluency 65
Long *a*: *ay*, *ai* 66

How Animals Grow
Farfallina & Marcel

Long *i*: *i*, *ie*, *igh*, *y* 67
Vocabulary 68
Comprehension: Inference Chart 69
Comprehension: Make Inferences 70
Fluency 71
Vocabulary Strategy: Synonyms 72
Long *i*; Contractions with *'s*, *'re*, *n't* 73
Text Feature: Illustrations and Captions 74

Staying Fit
There's Nothing Like
Baseball

Long *o*: *o*, *oa*, *ow*, *oe* 75
Vocabulary 76
Comprehension: Inference Chart 77
Comprehension: Make Inferences 78
Fluency 79
Vocabulary Strategy: Multiple-Meaning Words 80
Long *o*; Contractions with *'ll*, *'ve* 81
Text Feature: Graphs 82
Review Vocabulary 83
Review Vocabulary 84

© Macmillan/McGraw-Hill

Unit 3 • Better Together

Telling Stories
Head, Body, Legs:
A Story From Liberia

Long *e: e, ee, ea, y* 85
Vocabulary 86
Comprehension: Cause and Effect Chart 87
Comprehension: Cause and Effect 88
Fluency 89
Vocabulary Strategy: Context Clues 90
Long *e*; Suffixes *-ful, -less* 91
Text Feature: Drop-Down Menus 92

Safety First
Officer Buckle and Gloria

Long *u: u, u_e* 93
Vocabulary 94
Comprehension: Illustrations Chart 95
Comprehension: Use Illustrations 96
Fluency 97
Vocabulary Strategy: Synonyms 98
Long *u: u, u_e* 99
Text Feature: Floor Plan 100

Creatures Old
and Older
Time For Kids: Meet the
Super Croc

Consonant Digraphs: *ch, sh, th, wh* 101
Vocabulary 102
Comprehension: Summarize Chart 103
Comprehension: Summarize 104
Vocabulary Strategy: Suffixes and Prefixes 105
Study Skills: Narrow a Topic for Research 106
Fluency 107
Consonant Digraphs; Prefixes: *re-, un-, dis-* 108

Curtain Up!
The Alvin Ailey Kids:
Dancing As a Team

Consonant Digraphs: *ch, tch, ph, sh, th* 109
Vocabulary 110
Comprehension: Summarize Chart 111
Comprehension: Summarize 112
Fluency 113
Vocabulary Strategy: Antonyms 114
Consonant Digraphs; Open/Closed Syllables 115
Literary Elements: Alliteration and Rhythmic Patterns 116

On the Farm
Click, Clack, Moo:
Cows That Type

Triple Consonant Blends: *scr, spr, str* 117
Vocabulary 118
Comprehension: Cause and Effect Chart 119
Comprehension: Cause and Effect 120
Fluency 121
Vocabulary Strategy: Synonyms 122
Triple Consonant Blends; Possessives 123
Text Feature: Calendar 124
Review Vocabulary 125
Review Vocabulary 126

Unit 4 • Land, Sea, Sky

Animal Needs
Splish! Splash!
Animal Baths

r-Controlled Vowels: *ar, or* 127
Vocabulary 128
Comprehension: Compare and Contrast Chart 129
Comprehension: Compare and Contrast 130
Fluency 131
Vocabulary Strategy: Inflected Nouns 132
r-Controlled Vowels; Syllables 133
Literary Elements: Characters and Setting 134

Animal Survival
Goose's Story

r-Controlled Vowels: *er, ir, ur* 135
Vocabulary 136
Comprehension: Cause and Effect Chart 137
Comprehension: Cause and Effect 138
Fluency 139
Vocabulary Strategy: Comparatives and Superlatives 140
r-Controlled Vowels: *er, ir, ur* 141
Text Feature: Map 142

Helping Planet Earth
Time For Kids: A Way To
Help Planet Earth

Variant Vowels: *oo, ou* 143
Vocabulary 144
Comprehension: Description Web 145
Comprehension: Description 146
Vocabulary Strategy: Comparatives and Superlatives 147
Study Skill: Changes in Print 148
Fluency 149
Variant Vowels; Syllabication Rules
and Patterns 150

Wild Weather
Super Storms

Variant Vowels: *oo, ui, ew, oe, ue* 151
Vocabulary 152
Comprehension: Predictions Chart 153
Comprehension: Make and Confirm Predictions 154
Fluency 155
Vocabulary Strategy: Compound Words 156
Variant Vowels: *oo, ui, ew, oe, ue* 157
Literary Elements: Repetition and Word Choice 158

Habitats and Homes
Nutik, the Wolf Pup

Variant Vowels: *au, aw* 159
Vocabulary 160
Comprehension: Inference Chart 161
Comprehension: Make Inferences 162
Fluency 163
Vocabulary Strategy: Inflected Verbs and Base Words 164
Variant Vowels: *au, aw* 165
Text Feature: Heads 166
Review: Vocabulary 167
Review: Vocabulary 168

Unit 5 • Discoveries

Life in the Desert
Dig, Wait, Listen: A Desert Toad's Tale

Diphthong: *ou, ow* 169
Vocabulary 170
Comprehension: Author's Purpose Chart 171
Comprehension: Author's Purpose 172
Fluency 173
Vocabulary Strategy: Possessives. 174
Diphthong; Synonyms and Antonyms 175
Text Feature: Chart 176

Play Time!
Pushing Up the Sky

Diphthong: *oi, oy* 177
Vocabulary 178
Comprehension: Problem and Solution Chart 179
Comprehension: Problem and Solution. 180
Fluency 181
Vocabulary Strategy: Base Words, Inflected Endings 182
Diphthong; Homophones 183
Text Feature: Interview. 184

Exploration
Time For Kids: *Columbus Explores New Lands*

Schwa 185
Vocabulary 186
Comprehension: Main Idea and Details Web 187
Comprehension: Main Ideas and Details 188
Vocabulary Strategy: Classify and Categorize 189
Study Skill: Using the Internet 190
Fluency 191
Schwa; Derivations and Root Words 192

In the Garden
The Ugly Vegetables

Silent Consonants: *gn, kn, wr, mb* 193
Vocabulary 194
Comprehension: Sequence Chart 195
Comprehension: Sequence 196
Fluency 197
Vocabulary Strategy: Homophones. 198
Silent Consonants: *gn, kn, wr, mb* 199
Text Feature: Written Directions. 200

Our Moon
The Moon

Hard and Soft Consonants: *c, g*. 201
Vocabulary 202
Comprehension: Classify and Categorize Chart 203
Comprehension: Classify and Categorize. 204
Fluency 205
Vocabulary Strategy: Compound Words. 206
Hard and Soft Consonants: *c, g*. 207
Literary Elements: Personification and Imagery. 208
Review: Vocabulary 209
Review: Vocabulary 210

Unit 6 • Expressions

Count on a Celebration!
Mice and Beans

Endings *-dge, -ge, -lge, -nge, -rge* 211
Vocabulary 212
Comprehension: Fantasy and Reality Chart 213
Comprehension: Fantasy and Reality 214
Fluency 215
Vocabulary Strategy: Inflected Verbs 216
Endings *-dge, -ge, -lge, -nge, -rge* 217
Text Feature: Written Directions 218

Creating Stories
Stirring Up Memories

r-Controlled Vowel: *ar, are, air* 219
Vocabulary 220
Comprehension: Conclusion Chart 221
Comprehension: Draw Conclusions 222
Fluency 223
Vocabulary Strategy: Greek and Latin Roots 224
r-Controlled Vowel: *ar, are, air* 225
Literary Elements: Onomatopoeia and Word Play 226

Worlds of Art
Time For Kids: *Music of the Stone Age*

r-Controlled Vowel: *er, eer, ere, ear* 227
Vocabulary 228
Comprehension: Make Judgments Chart 229
Comprehension: Make Judgments 230
Vocabulary Strategy: Multiple-Meaning Words 231
Study Skills: Choosing Research Materials 232
Fluency 233
r-Controlled Vowel: *er, eer, ere, ear* 234

Inventors Then and Now
African-American Inventors

r-Controlled Vowel: *or, ore, oar* 235
Vocabulary 236
Comprehension: Compare and Contrast Chart 237
Comprehension: Compare and Contrast 238
Fluency 239
Vocabulary Strategy: Suffixes 240
r-Controlled Vowel; Related Words 241
Text Feature: Time Line 242

Other People, Other Places
Babu's Song

r-Controlled Vowel: *ire, ier, ure* 243
Vocabulary 244
Comprehension: Character and Setting Chart 245
Comprehension: Character and Setting 246
Fluency 247
Vocabulary Strategy: Syntactic and Semantic Cues 248
r-Controlled Vowel; Related Words 249
Text Feature: Map 250
Review Vocabulary 251
Review Vocabulary 252

© Macmillan/McGraw-Hill

Name _____

As you read *David's New Friends*, fill in the
Character and Setting Chart.

Character	Setting

How does the information you wrote in this Character
and Setting Chart help you analyze story structure in
David's New Friends?

At Home: Have your child use the chart to retell the story.

David's New Friends
Book 2.1/U

3

Name _____

The **characters** are the people or animals in a story.

The **setting** is where and when a story happens.

Read the passage below. Then write the answers to each question on the line.

It was the first day of school. Tim was worried. He saw the large playground and lots of children. He wondered if he would make new friends. When Tim heard the bell ring, he walked to his classroom. He sat at a desk next to a boy named Rob. Rob asked Tim if he would like to be friends. Tim was excited to have a new friend.

1. Who are the characters in the passage? _____

2. What is each character like?

_____

3. What is the setting of this passage? _____

_____

4. Write two sentences about your first day of school.

_____

_____

 At Home: Have your child write a short story with a character and a setting.

As I read, I will pay attention to punctuation in each sentence.

	"It's nearly time for our school fair," said Mr. Jeffs.
10	"What is our class doing?" asked Lucy.
17	"We could grow vegetables in our garden," said Sam.
26	"Then we could sell them," said Chico.
33	"It's too late," said Mr. Jeffs. "Potatoes, beans, and
42	carrots need time to grow."
47	Jing took a deep breath. "We could grow sprouts,"
56	she whispered.
58	"Sprouts?" said Mr. Jeffs. "That sounds interesting, Jing."
66	"We grow sprouts at home," said Jing. "They're ready
75	to eat in a few days."
81	"Sprouts!" Everyone was excited. "We'll grow sprouts!" 88

Comprehension Check

1. How can you tell that Jing is shy? **Character and Setting**

2. Why is Jing's solution a good idea? **Draw Conclusions**

	Words Read	–	Number of Errors	=	Words Correct Score
First Read		–		=	
Second Read		–		=	

At Home: Help your child read the passage, paying attention to the goal at the top of the page.

David's New Friends
Book 2.1/Unit 1

5

Dictionary entries are listed in **alphabetical order**. To help you put words in alphabetical order, think about where you would find them in the dictionary.

Write the following groups of words in alphabetical order.

1. friend _____
   trust _____
   nice _____

2. share _____
   caring _____
   sweet _____

3. dog _____
   game _____
   bed _____

4. love _____
   ice _____
   jump _____

5. teacher _____
   school _____
   principal _____

6. recess _____
   reading _____
   math _____

 At Home: Write six to eight words and have your child put them in alphabetical order.

☐ **Practice**

Short *a* and *i*,
Inflectional Endings
-s and *-es*

Name _____

> Short **a** is the middle sound heard in **trap** and **map.**
>
> Short **i** is the middle sound heard in **sit** and **pick.**
>
> Use **-s** or **-es** to make some words mean more than one.

Read each sentence. Then complete the sentence with one of the words from the list below it.

1. Please put all your _____ in the sink.
dish   dishs   dishes

2. Ken has three baseball _____.
bats   bat   bates

3. Which one of these _____ would you like?
cat   cats   cates

4. Laura has two _____ on her farm.
piges   pig   pigs

5. The baby gave me two wet _____ on the cheek.
kisses   kisss   kiss

6. My cat likes to take four _____ a day.
napes   naps   nap

 At Home: Have your child name two words that have the
short *a* and *i* sounds.

David's New Friends
Book 2.1/Unit 1

7

Name _____

Captions are the words below a picture. They tell what the picture is about or explain what the people in it are saying or doing.

I. **Write a caption to go with this picture.**

_____

2. **Read the caption and draw a picture to go with it.**

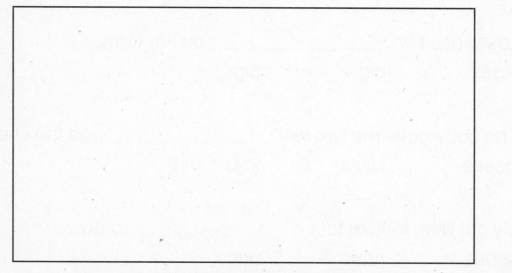

Recess is my favorite time of day.

At Home: Have your child draw a picture and write a caption for it.

As I read, I will pay attention to punctuation and how it affects expression.

	"Where does this path go?" asked Jasmine.
7	Just then, a butterfly flew past. It went down
16	the path.
18	"We should follow it!" said Jasmine.
24	"Okay," said Dad.
27	Jasmine pulled him up.
31	The butterfly led Jasmine and her dad into
39	a field.
41	"Wow!" she said. They saw a big bush. It was
51	covered in purple flowers and butterflies.
57	A woman was kneeling next to the bush.
65	"Excuse me," said Jasmine. "Why do butterflies
72	love this bush?"
75	"It is a butterfly bush," said the woman. 83

Comprehension Check

1. Why does Jasmine follow the butterfly? **Plot**

2. What do you think the woman is doing? **Make Inferences**

	Words Read	−	Number of Errors	=	Words Correct Score
First Read		−		=	
Second Read		−		=	

At Home: Help your child read the passage, paying attention to the goal at the top of the page.

Mr. Putter & Tabby Pour the Tea
Book 2.1/Unit 1

Name _____

> Verbs can have different **word endings.** These groups of letters tell when something happens.

Underline the word that completes each sentence. Write the word on the line. Then circle the sentences that tell about the past.

1. Josie is always _____ to new people.
   talked   talking

2. After school, Jen _____ home with her new friends.
   walking   walked

3. Tim and Sam are still _____ outside.
   playing   played

4. Tammy _____ her mom if she could come over to my house.
   asking   asked

5. Grandma _____ the flowers I gave her.
   saved   saving

6. Lisa is _____ for Jim on the soccer field.
   waited   waiting

At Home: For each question above, have your child make up a sentence using one of the inflections not chosen as the answer.

Practice

Short *o, e, u,*
Inflectional Endings
-ing and *-ed*

Name _____

> Before adding **-ing** to some verbs with short vowels,
> double the final consonant.

A. Add *-ing* to each word. Then use each new word in a sentence.

I. run _____

_____

2. hop _____

_____

3. get _____

_____

B. Add *-ed* to each word. Then use each new word in a sentence.

4. lock _____

_____

5. help _____

_____

6. jump _____

_____

At Home: Have your child suggest other words that have the
sounds of short *e*, short *o*, and short *u*. Then have him or her
use each one in an oral sentence.

A **list** is a number of things written down in a certain order or grouping.

Read the list of rules. Then use the rules to answer each question below.

Park Rules

- Throw trash in trash cans.
- Be kind to friends and others in the playground.
- Do not play in the playground after dark.
- Do not let pets go close to swings and slides.

1. Juan has just finished eating his lunch. What should he do with the empty bags?

_____

2. The sun has gone down. Is it okay for Mai Lee to play on a swing? Why or why not?

_____

_____

3. Gina is walking her dog on the sidewalk. She wants to talk to a friend who is on the slide. What should she do? Why?

_____

_____

4. Write another rule you think would be helpful at the park.

_____

At Home: Ask your child to write a list of at least three classroom rules and explain why each one is important.

© Macmillan/McGraw-Hill

As I read, I will pay attention to the punctuation and pronunciation of vocabulary words.

	Fire can be dangerous. But it is also very useful.
10	People use fire every day. Sometimes they use fire
19	without even knowing it.
23	Some people have a fireplace at home. Fireplaces
31	burn wood, gas, or coal. Some can now be turned on
42	with the touch of a button.
48	People also use fire at home to cook. Many kitchen
58	stoves burn gas. Others are electric. Electric burners turn
67	red when they are hot, but you will not see **flames**. 78

Comprehension Check

I. Why is fire important? **Main Idea and Details**

2. What are two ways people use fire in their homes? **Main Idea and Details**

	Words Read	–	Number of Errors	=	Words Correct Score
First Read		–		=	
Second Read		–		=	

At Home: Help your child read the passage, paying attention to the goal at the top of the page.

Fighting the Fire • Book 2.1/Unit I   23

© Macmillan/McGraw-Hill

A. Write a word from the box to complete each sentence. Then circle the words that have the short *a* sound.

came	hat	gave	class

A fireman _____ to our _____ today. He

_____ us some great safety tips. After his speech, he let

Mrs. Jacobs wear his firefighter _____.

You can add the suffixes **-er** and **-est** to make comparisons.

The suffix **-er** means "more than."
The suffix **-est** means "most."

B. Add *-er* or *-est* to the words in the box to complete each sentence.

fast	loud	small	strong

The fire trucks drove _____ than the cars on the

road. The sirens were the _____ I have ever heard.

The chief told the _____ firefighter to carry up the

heavy hose. Soon the flames became _____, and

the fire was put out.

At Home: Help your child identify words with the suffixes
-er and *-est* in a newspaper article. Discuss how the suffix
changes the meaning of the base word.

© Macmillan/McGraw-Hill

Name _____

As you read *Meet Rosina*, fill in the Main Idea and
Details Web.

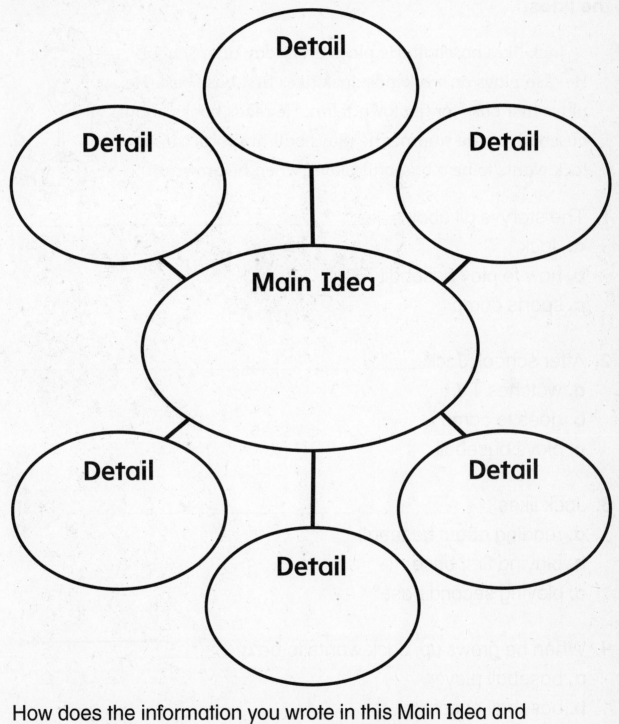

How does the information you wrote in this Main Idea and
Details Web help you summarize *Meet Rosina*?

At Home: Have your child use the chart to retell the story.

Read the passage. Circle the word or group of words that complete each sentence. Then write the answers on the lines.

Jack likes baseball. He plays every day after school. He also plays on weekends. Jack likes first base best. He plays first base for the town team. He reads books about baseball. In the summer he plays ball at sports camp. Jack wants to be a baseball player when he grows up.

1. The story is all about _____.
   a. Jack
   b. how to play baseball
   c. sports camp

2. After school, Jack _____.
   a. watches TV
   b. goes to camp
   c. plays baseball

3. Jack likes _____ best.
   a. reading about baseball
   b. playing first base
   c. playing second base

4. When he grows up, Jack wants to be a _____.
   a. baseball player
   b. baseball coach
   c. sports writer

At Home: Ask your child: If this story were about you and what you like, what would it be all about? Have your child dictate his or her story to you. Then have your child identify the main idea.

As I read, I will pay attention to the pronunciation of the vocabulary words.

9	People who are deaf cannot hear. They need to talk and listen without using sounds.
15	**Deaf** people communicate in many ways.
21	A language that is often used by deaf people is
31	called **sign language.**
34	Sign language uses signs for words. Signs are
42	made using hand shapes and movements.
48	One way to sign is to spell out a word. There is
60	a sign for each letter of the alphabet.
68	Another way to sign is to show a whole word. 78

Comprehension Check

1. What is this passage about? **Main Idea and Details**

2. How do people use signs to communicate? **Main Idea and Details**

	Words Read	–	Number of Errors	=	Words Correct Score
First Read		–		=	
Second Read		–		=	

At Home: Help your child read the passage, paying attention to the goal at the top of the page.

A **dictionary** lists words and their meanings. Some words have more than one meaning.

Use the dictionary definition to find the correct definition for the word *sign* in each sentence. Write the number of the definition on the line. Then write if *sign* is used as a *noun* or *verb*.

ONE WAY

sign (sine) *noun* **1.** A symbol that means or stands for something: *This sign means add:* +. **2.** Something written, such as a poster, that gives information: *This sign means the street goes one way.*
verb **3.** To write your name: *Please sign on the dotted line.*
4. To use American Sign Language: *I can sign the word* dog.

1. That movie star will <u>sign</u> pictures for her fans.

   In this sentence, *sign* means _____

2. The <u>sign</u> says we should turn left.

   In this sentence, *sign* means _____

3. They <u>sign</u> to each other across the room.

   In this sentence, *sign* means _____

4. This is the <u>sign</u> for cents ¢.

   In this sentence, *sign* means _____

At Home: Help your child use each meaning for the word *sign* in a sentence of his or her own.

Practice

Short and Long *i*,
Inflectional Endings
-ed and *-ing*

Name _____

> The letters *-ing* and *-ed* can be added to the end of a verb to change its meaning.
>
> If a word ends in silent *e,* drop the *e* before adding *-ing* or *-ed.*
>
> smile − e + ed = smiled   shine − e + ing = shining

A. Add *-ing* to the end of each word. Write the new word.
Then use the word in a sentence.

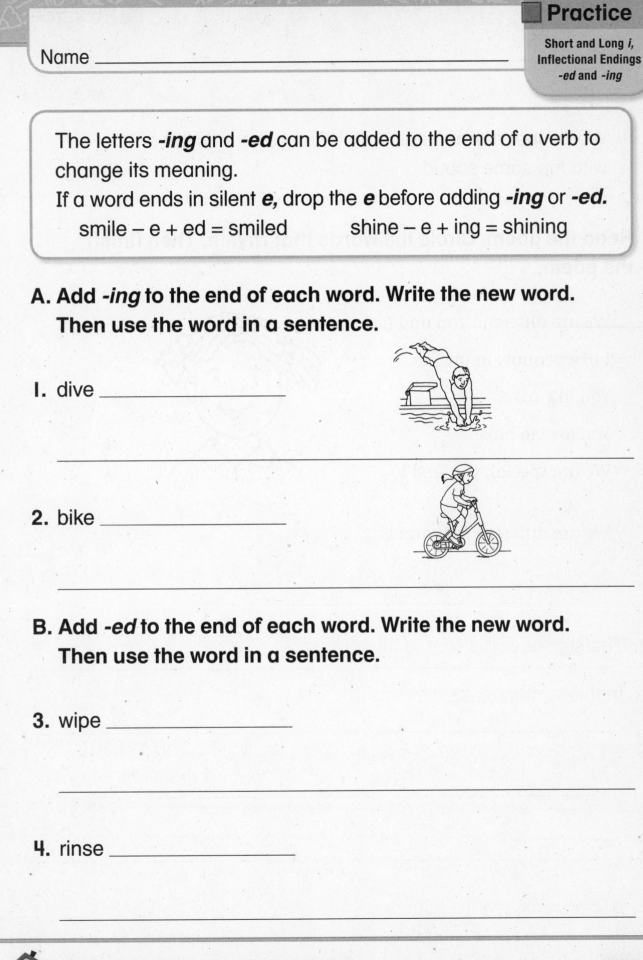

1. dive _____

_____

2. bike _____

_____

B. Add *-ed* to the end of each word. Write the new word.
Then use the word in a sentence.

3. wipe _____

_____

4. rinse _____

_____

© Macmillan/McGraw-Hill

At Home: Have a spelling bee. Show your child the following words: *hide, make, take,* and *ride.* Then ask him or her to add *-ing* and spell the word aloud.

Meet Rosina • Book 2.1/Unit 1   **31**

Name _____

Words that **rhyme** begin with different sounds but end
with the same sound.

**Read the poem. Circle the words that rhyme. Then finish
the poem.**

We are different, you and I.

I like peanuts in my pie.

You like cake.

You love to bake.

We are special, you and I.

We are different, you and I.

_____

_____

_____

_____

At Home: Have your child write a rhyming poem about how
he or she is special.

Name _____

A. Match each word to its meaning. Then write the letter of the meaning on the line.

1. cuddle _____   **a.** protected

2. wrinkled _____   **b.** warmth or hotness

3. heat _____   **c.** made lines in

4. delighted _____   **d.** hug

5. flames _____   **e.** pleased

6. safe _____   **f.** fire

B. Write the word from the box that completes each sentence.

| yams | vase | groan | language | fog | rim |

1. Ella put the flowers in a _____.

2. Dad had trouble finding his way in the thick _____.

3. The _____ of the cup was chipped.

4. I like _____ better than white potatoes.

5. Our trip to Germany was hard because we didn't speak the

   _____.

6. The boys _____ when they have to go to bed early.

Name _____

Choose a word from the box to complete each sentence. Then write the answers in the puzzle.

excited	tomorrow	company	enjoyed
well	celebrate	deaf	settled

Across

1. If you move to a new house, it will take time for you to feel

   _____.

5. People who come to your house to visit are _____.

6. The opposite of sick is _____.

7. You feel _____ when you know something fun will happen.

Down

2. If you had a good time,

   you _____ yourself.

3. The day after today

   is _____.

4. Someone who cannot hear

   is _____.

5. How do you _____

   birthdays and holidays?

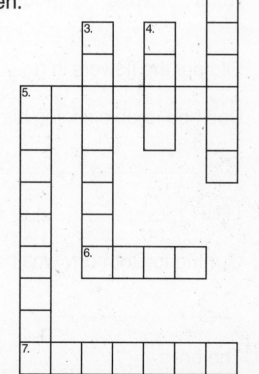

Name _____

The *u* in *cup* stands for the short *u* sound.

The *u* in *cube* stands for the long *u* sound.

Circle the word that completes each sentence. Then write the word on the line.

1. Chewing _____ is not good for your teeth.
   gum   glue   tube

2. Planting seeds is a lot of _____.
   hug   fume   fun

3. Keith is learning to play the _____.
   fuse   flute   fluff

4. Everyone needs to follow the class _____.
   shut   rules   run

5. The _____ carried food to the stores.
   chunk   trust   truck

6. The ice _____ melted.
   cute   cube   cub

7. The _____ has a bad odor when it lifts its tail.
   skunk   stink   fume

8. Mary squeezed the _____ of toothpaste.
   tub   tube   huge

© Macmillan/McGraw-Hill

At Home: Help your child suggest other words that have the sounds for short and long *u*. Have him or her use each word in a sentence.

The Tiny Seed • **Book 2.1/Unit 2**   43

A. Match each meaning with the correct word. Write the letter of the meaning on the line.

1. burst _____   **a.** floats or moves along by wind

2. gently _____   **b.** hot, dry, sandy area of land

3. drifts _____   **c.** person living near another

4. drowns _____   **d.** to break open, suddenly

5. neighbor _____   **e.** carefully

6. desert _____   **f.** to die by staying underwater

B. Choose two words. Use each one in a sentence. Write the sentences on the lines below.

7. _____

_____

8. _____

_____

As you read *The Tiny Seed*, fill in the Conclusion Chart

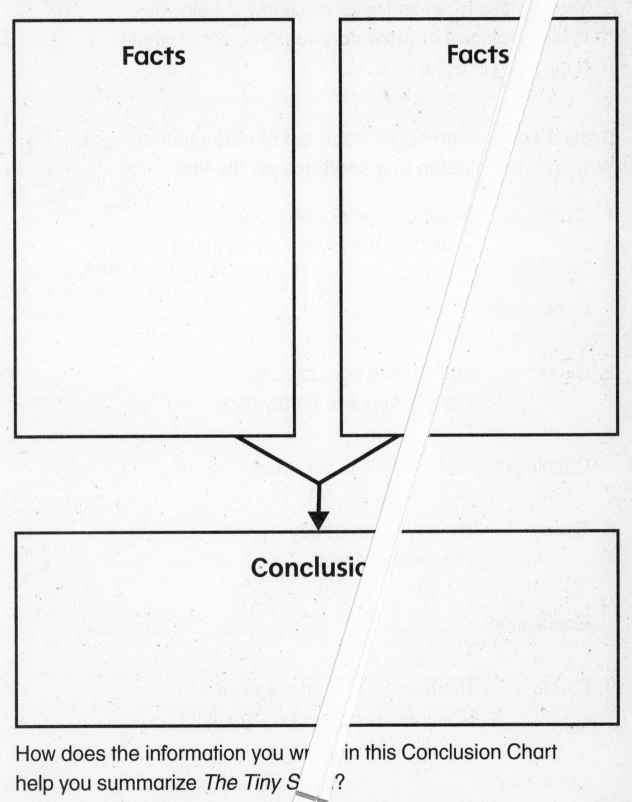

Facts

Facts

Conclusion

How does the information you wrote in this Conclusion Chart help you summarize *The Tiny Seed*?

 At Home: Have your child use the chart to retell the ...

Name _____

You can use clues and what you know to help you make decisions, or **draw conclusions,** about what is happening in a story.

Draw a conclusion about each set of clues below. Write the conclusion in a sentence on the line.

1. Clues: Mike has a pair of scissors.
                Now there are fewer flowers in the garden.

Conclusion: _____

2. Clues: Sarah had a pack of seeds.
                The seed pack is empty now.

Conclusion: _____

3. Clues: The sky looks cloudy.
                The ground is wet.

Conclusion: _____

4. Clues: There was a bud on the plant.
                Now there is a flower on the plant.

Conclusion: _____

 At Home: Have your child make up his or her own clues for you to draw a conclusion. Discuss the words that helped you draw a conclusion.

© Macmillan/McGraw-Hill

As I read, I will pay attention to the punctuation in each sentence.

7	The raffia palm (PAHLM) has the longest leaves of any plant. One leaf can be as long as a school
19	bus.
20	The leaves of the giant taro plant are also huge.
30	They look like elephant ears. But the largest leaf
39	ever is even bigger than an elephant's body!
47	A rafflesia has giant petals. These flowers can be
56	as wide as you are tall!
62	Some plants have giant seeds. The coco-de-mer
69	palm has seeds that are heavier than two bowling
78	balls. 79

Comprehension Check

1. How can you tell that the coco-de-mer seeds are heavy? **Draw Conclusions**

2. How are the plants in the passage alike? **Compare and Contrast**

	Words Read	–	Number of Errors	=	Words Correct Score
First Read		–		=	
Second Read		–		=	

© Macmillan/McGraw-Hill

At Home: Help your child read the passage, paying attention to the goal at the top of the page.

Context clues are words in a sentence or a story that can help you figure out the meaning of a word you don't know. They can come before or after the new word.

Read each sentence. Look at the word in dark print. Underline the context clues that help you figure out what the word in dark print means. Then write what you think each word means.

1. With sunlight and water, a seed can **mature** into a plant.

_____

2. Tim dug a hole in the **earth** and placed the seed in it.

_____

3. The **veins** in the leaf looked like a spiderweb.

_____

4. Lisa thought the **gigantic** seed would grow into a big plant.

_____

5. Omar was so **excited** that the plant had grown that he cheered.

_____

 At Home: Ask your child to find a sentence in a book with a new word and use context clues to tell what the word means.

© Macmillan/McGraw-Hill

Name _____

A. Circle the correct word to complete each sentence. Then write it on the line.

1. My dad took _____ to the park.
   us   use

2. The little baby was very _____.
   cute   cut

3. The bear _____ ran to its mother.
   cube   cub

> The *-er* ending means "more."   The *-est* ending means "most."
>
> fast + **er** = faster (more fast)   fastest + **est** = fastest (most fast)

B. Circle the correct word to complete each sentence. Then write it on the line.

4. Molly planted the _____ seed of them all.
   smaller   smallest

5. She planted two _____ seeds.
   largest   larger

6. Which plant grew the _____?
   tallest   taller

© Macmillan/McGraw-Hill

 At Home: Have your child add *-er* and *-est* to five words and write a sentence for each word.

Name _____

> **Diagrams** are drawings that give information. **Labels** tell more about a diagram.

Look at the diagram. Read the labels. Then answer the questions below.

The Parts of a Pine Tree

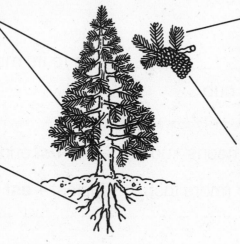

Branches and **trunk** carry water and food to different parts of the tree.

Roots take water from the soil.

Needles make food for the tree. They stay green all year.

Cones hold the tree's seeds.

I. What does this diagram show? _____

2. Which part makes food for the tree? _____

3. What do cones do? _____

4. What carries water and food? _____

5. How does the diagram show what the roots look like?

_____

At Home: Have your child draw his or her own diagram of a tree or plant and label its parts.

Name _____

Sometimes two **consonants** form a blend. In a consonant blend, you can hear the sound of each consonant.

Listen for the **blends** at the beginning of these words.

spoon

sky

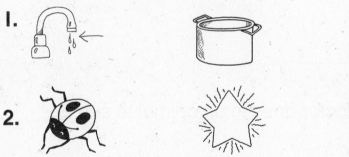

Listen for the **blends** at the end of these words.

toa**st**

ma**sk**

A. Circle the two pictures in each row whose names have the same beginning blend.

1.

2.

B. Circle the two pictures in each row whose names have the same blend at the end.

3.

4.

 At Home: Ask your child to choose the name of one of the pictures and use it in a sentence.

A Harbor Seal Pup Grows Up
Book 2.1/Unit 2

51

Name _____

Choose a word from the box to answer each question.
Write the word on the line.

| young normal rescued examines mammal hunger |

1. What is another word for **saved**? _____

2. Which word names a kind of animal that drinks its mother's milk and has

   hair or fur? _____

3. Which word best tells about someone

   who is not old? _____

4. Which word tells what a doctor does to an animal to see if

   it is well? _____

5. Which word tells about the feeling an animal has when it needs

   to eat? _____

6. Which word tells about something that is not odd?

   _____

Name _____

As you read *A Harbor Seal Pup Grows Up*, fill in the
Sequence Chart.

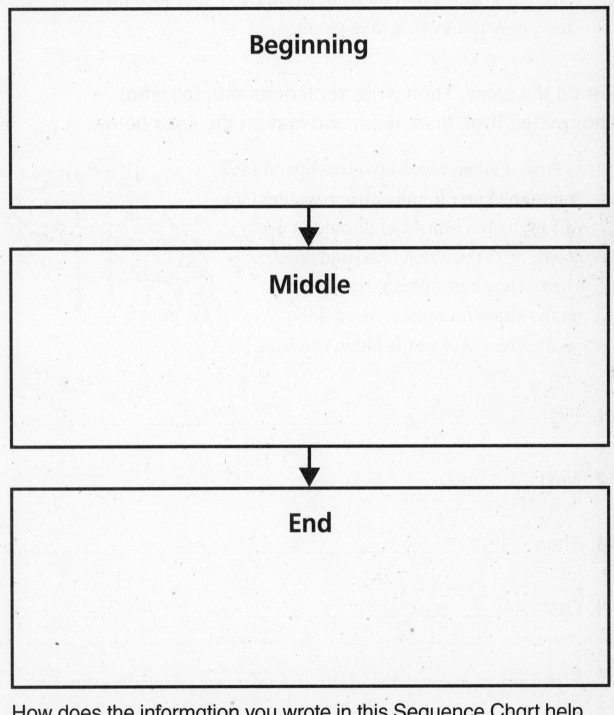

Beginning

Middle

End

How does the information you wrote in this Sequence Chart help
you summarize *A Harbor Seal Pup Grows Up*?

© Macmillan/McGraw-Hill

 At Home: Have your child use the chart to retell the story.

A Harbor Seal Pup Grows Up
Book 2.1/Unit 2

53

The **sequence** of events is the order of which things happen. Words such as *first, then, next,* and *last* give clues to when events take place.

Read the story. Then write sentences that tell what happened first, then, next, and last on the lines below.

First, a kitten raced up a tree after a bird. Before she knew it, the kitten was stuck. She was high on a branch and couldn't get down. Next the kitten cried and cried. Then, a boy came along. He scooped up the kitten and placed her gently on the grass. At last the kitten was safe.

1. First _____

2. Next _____

3. Then _____

4. Last _____

_____

At Home: Have your child use the words *first, then, next,* and *last* to tell you what happened at school today.

As I read, I will pay attention to the pronunciation of vocabulary words.

9	All tigers have stripes. But each tiger has different stripes.
10	Tigers live in jungles and forests. A tiger's coat
19	helps it blend in with long grass, bushes, and trees.
29	This helps keep the tiger safe.
35	Tigers are mammals. A **mammal** feeds its
42	**young** on milk. Tiger cubs live with their mother for
52	two to three years. Adult male tigers live alone.
61	Tigers hunt alone. They hide, and then sneak up
70	on their prey. They catch deer, wild pigs, and cattle. 80

Comprehension Check

I. How does a tiger's diet change as it grows up? **Sequence**

2. How do stripes help a tiger? **Main Idea and Details**

	Words Read	–	Number of Errors	=	Words Correct Score
First Read		–		=	
Second Read		–		=	

© Macmillan/McGraw-Hill

 At Home: Help your child read the passage, paying attention to the goal at the top of the page.

A Harbor Seal Pup Grows Up
Book 2.1/Unit 2 55

> **Antonyms** are words that have opposite or almost opposite meanings.

Circle the antonyms in each pair of sentences. Then write them on the line.

1. I remember my first animal rescue. _____

   I knew it would not be my last. _____

2. My neighbor lost her puppy. _____

   I found him the next day. _____

3. The puppy did not go very far. _____

   He was near the park behind my house. _____

4. The puppy was shaking from the cold. _____

   His fur could not keep him warm in all the snow. _____

5. I bent down to see if the puppy was alright. _____

   He let me pick him up to carry him home. _____

 At Home: Ask your child to tell you other antonym pairs and use them in sentences.

Name _____

A. Choose a word from the word box that has the same beginning or ending blend as each of the words below. Write the word on the line.

skunk   drop   spill   spoon   mask   best   sleep

I. drain _____   3. slow _____   5. sky _____

2. spark _____   4. task _____   6. nest _____

A **compound word** is a word made up of two smaller words.

up + stairs = upstairs   week + end = weekend

B. Put a word from the box with each word below to make a compound word. Write the compound word on the line.

pack   box   corn   fall

7. water _____   9. back _____

8. mail _____   10. pop _____

At Home: Ask your child why *horseback* is
a compound word.

A Harbor Seal Pup Grows Up
Book 2.1/Unit 2
57

© Macmillan/McGraw-Hill

> **Similes** compare one thing to another. It uses the words *like* or *as*.

Read each question. Answer it with a complete sentence that includes the underlined simile from the question. Then draw a picture to show what is happening in the sentence.

1. When might a person be <u>as hungry as a bear</u>?

_____

_____

_____
| |
| |
| |
| |
_____

2. What might people be doing when they are <u>as busy as bees</u>?

_____

_____

_____
| |
| |
| |
| |
| |
_____

 At Home: Have your child answer this question:
"When might someone work like a dog?"

The letters *ai* and *ay* can stand for the long *a* sound.
Listen for the long *a* sound as you say the word *braid*.
Listen for the long *a* sound as you say the word *day*.

Read each sentence. Then write the letters *ai* or *ay* on the lines to complete each word.

1. Tod_____ I will go to the doctor.

2. Dad and I will take a tr_____n there.

3. Dad said I could p_____ the clerk for the train tickets.

4. He will w_____t with me in the doctor's office.

5. Mom m_____ come, too.

6. A sitter will st_____ with my little sister.

7. Mom has p_____d the sitter already.

8. We'll read our m_____l when we get home.

At Home: Ask your child to suggest other words that have
the long *a* sound spelled *ai* or *ay*.

Name _____

Choose a word from the box to complete the letter.

| serious | broken | personal | informs | heal |

Dear María,

I have big news! I fell next to the pool at

camp and now I have a _____

arm. The fall was very _____, but

the doctors told me I will _____

quickly. My family came for a visit as soon as

they found out. They got here in just a few hours.

When a kid is hurt, the hospital always

_____ parents right away. The

camp let me have a _____ day

so I could visit with my family. I am staying at

camp until it is over, but no more swimming for

me! Let me know how you are.

Your friend always,

Ricky

Choose one of the words from the box to write a P.S. to the letter.

P.S.: _____

_____

Name _____

As you read *A Trip to the Emergency Room*, fill in the Sequence Chart.

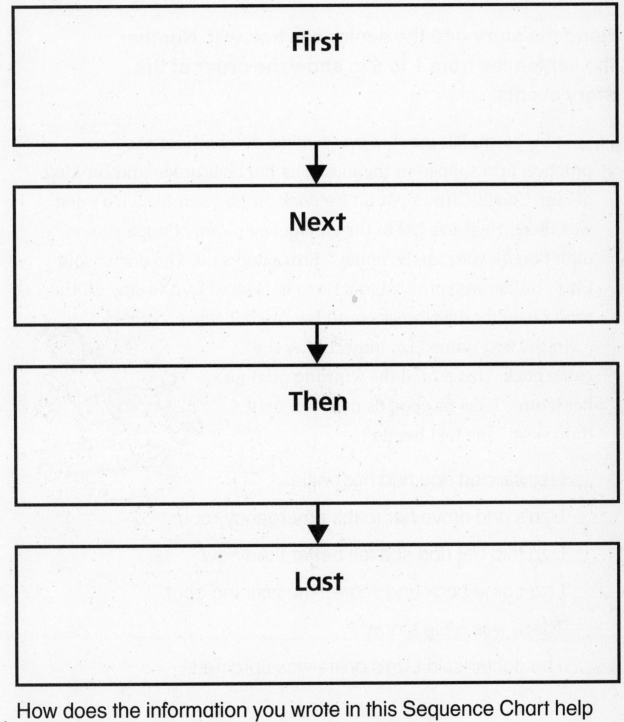

First

↓

Next

↓

Then

↓

Last

How does the information you wrote in this Sequence Chart help you summarize *A Trip to the Emergency Room*?

 At Home: Have your child use the chart to retell the story.

Sequence is the order in which events happen in a story.

Read the story and the sentences below it. Number the sentences from 1 to 6 to show the order of the story events.

A big storm left puddles everywhere. After school at soccer practice, Liza slipped in the mud. She hurt her ankle and couldn't get up. Coach Grimes put an ice pack on Liza's ankle. Liza's dad was there. He drove her to the emergency room. "I hope you didn't break your ankle, honey," Liza's dad said. The doctor said Liza's ankle was sprained, not broken. He told Liza to stay off the soccer field for a few weeks until her ankle healed.

In the first game Liza played after she came back, Liza scored the winning goal for her team. "I feel as good as new. No, better than new!" she told her dad.

_____ Liza slipped and hurt her ankle.

_____ Liza's dad drove her to the emergency room.

_____ Liza told her dad she felt better than new.

_____ Liza came back and scored the winning goal.

_____ There was a big storm.

_____ The doctor said Liza's ankle was sprained.

© Macmillan/McGraw-Hill

At Home: Have your child tell about six events from his or her day at school in the order in which they happened.

Homophones are words that sound the same, but have different meanings and different spellings. When you come to a new word that sounds the same as another word you know, you can use a dictionary to look up the word's meaning.

Study the dictionary entries. Then write a new sentence for each homophone.

> **knows** *verb* is aware of or understands something. *Alex knows that summer begins in June.*

> **nose** *noun* the part of the face we breathe and smell with. *The boy covered his nose before he sneezed.*

1. _____

2. _____

> **weak** *adjective* not strong. *Grandma was weak during her illness.*

> **week** *noun* a period of seven days in a row. *We went on vacation for a week.*

3. _____

4. _____

© Macmillan/McGraw-Hill

At Home: Have your child write sentences using the homophones *right* and *write*. If a dictionary is available, help your child look up the meaning of each word before he or she writes the sentences.

The library's **card catalog** and other **reference sources** have many different kinds of information.

Match each reference source to its description below. Write the letter of the description on the line.

I. card catalog ___

2. almanac ___

3. atlas ___

4. newspaper ___

5. globe ___

6. telephone directory ___

a. a model of Earth with labeled countries and bodies of water

b. a daily or weekly publication containing news about current events

c. a book of maps and information about different geographical areas

d. a book that lists people and businesses alphabetically, along with their addresses and phone numbers

e. an alphabetical listing of books in a library, on computer or index cards

f. a yearly book containing a variety of practical information

Read each item. Write the answer to the question.

7. You want to know where Italy is. What are two good places

to look? _____

8. You need a book about nursing. Where should you look?

_____

© Macmillan/McGraw-Hill

At Home: Ask your child what library resource he or she would use to find the following: a book about doctors, a list of national holidays, and the shape of the continent Africa.

As I read, I will pay attention to the pronunciation of vocabulary words.

9	Your body is working even when you are just sitting still. You can see, hear, smell, taste, and feel.
19	Your body knows when it is cold or hot. It can
30	even **heal** itself when a part is **broken** or you feel
41	sick.
42	Sometimes a doctor can help your body get well.
51	A doctor can also give you a **personal** checkup
60	once a year to be sure you stay healthy.
69	Let's take a look at the human body. Then
78	we will see how a doctor can help you keep it
89	healthy. 90

Comprehension Check

1. Does your body always need a doctor to get well? **Make Inferences**

2. How do you know that your body is working even when you are still? **Make and Confirm Predictions**

	Words Read	–	Number of Errors	=	Words Correct Score
First Read		–		=	
Second Read		–		=	

At Home: Help your child read the passage, paying attention to the goal at the top of the page.

A Trip to the Emergency Room
Book 2.1/Unit 2

65

The long *a* sound can be spelled with the letters *ai* and *ay.* You can hear the long *a* sound in *main* and the long *a* sound in *way.*

**Circle a word to complete each sentence.
Then write the word on the line.**

1. Sam put some oats in a _____.

   pain   pail   may

2. Then he grabbed a bundle of _____.

   stay   nail   hay

3. Sam fed the _____ horse.

   gray   day   rain

4. Then he brushed the horse's _____.

   tray   tail   raid

5. Kelly wrote a letter about biking on a mountain _____.

   paid   gain   trail

6. Kelly put the letter in the _____.

   mail   say   wait

 At Home: Work with your child to make up rhymes with words that have long *a* spelled *ai* or *ay.*

Name _____

The long *i* sound can be spelled with the letters *i, ie, igh,* or *y.*

Choose a word from the box to complete each sentence.

why	climb	light	blind
tie	fly	high	pie

1. We like to _____ trees.

2. The street _____ shines in my window at night.

3. Dad likes apple _____ with raisins.

4. My friend has a seeing-eye dog. She is _____.

5. Mr. Simon wears a _____ with his suit.

6. The geese _____ south every year.

7. Ask if you want to know _____.

8. How _____ is that kite?

© Macmillan/McGraw-Hill

 At Home: Have your child suggest other words that have the long *i* sound spelled *i, ie, igh,* and *y.* Then ask him or her to use the words in oral sentences.

Farfallina & Marcel
Book 2.1/Unit 2
67

Name _____

A. Write the word from the box that matches each clue.

peered   giggled   snuggled   fluttered   vanished   recognized

I. This word means "held something close" or "cuddled."

_____

2. This word means "disappeared" or "went out of sight."

_____

3. This word means "laughed in a silly way."

_____

4. This word means "knew by sight."

_____

5. This word means "flew with quick flapping movements."

_____

6. This word means "looked closely."

_____

B. Choose two words from the box. Then write a sentence for each word that you chose on the lines.

_____

_____

Name _____

As you read *Farfallina & Marcel,* fill in the
Inference Chart.

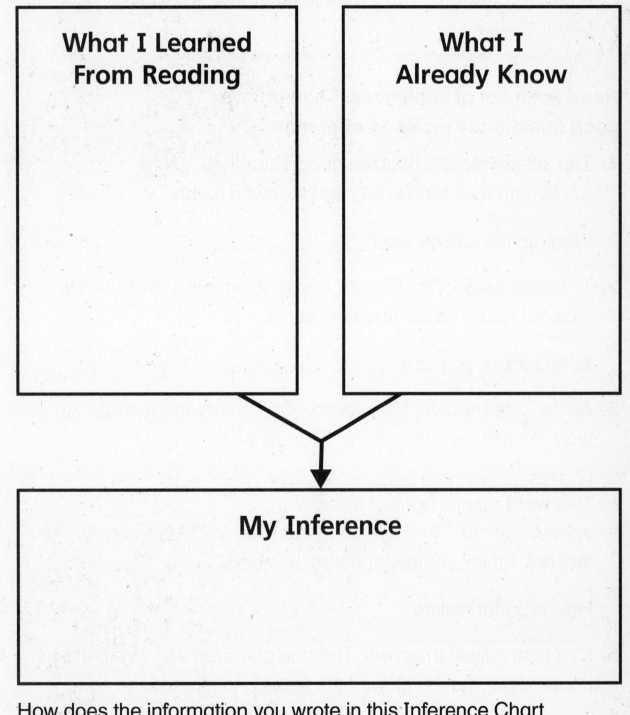

**What I Learned
From Reading**

**What I
Already Know**

My Inference

How does the information you wrote in this Inference Chart
help you to better understand *Farfallina and Marcel*?

 At Home: Have your child use the chart to retell the story.

When you **make inferences**, you use what you already know and what you have read to figure out something about a story.

Read each set of sentences. Then answer each question to make an inference.

I. The kittens met Mary at the door. Then they ran over to their food bowls and meowed loudly.

What do the kittens want? _____

2. Ty stored his shorts, T-shirts, and bathing suit in a chest. He took out his sweaters and long pants.

What time of year is it? _____

3. All the kids lined up. Max yelled, "Go!" Everyone ran fast. Amy won. "That's my sister, Amy!" Max yelled.

How does Max feel about his sister? _____

4. Janet sneezed. Then she coughed. Dad felt her forehead. "You feel hot. I think you better go back to bed."

How is Janet feeling? _____

5. Mr. Night milked the cows. Then he gathered eggs from the hen house. After that he plowed the fields and planted the corn.

Where does Mr. Night work? _____

© Macmillan/McGraw-Hill

At Home: Encourage your child to make another inference for each story.

As I read, I will pay attention to the punctuation in each sentence and tempo.

	My name is Hermie. My mother was a land hermit
10	crab. She laid her eggs on the wet rocks next to the sea.
23	When I hatched, I floated in the warm ocean. I saw
34	many other baby hermit crabs there. That is where I met
45	my friend Harriet.
48	As we grew, we molted. We slipped out of the hard
59	skin around our body.
63	When we had molted for the last time, we knew it was
75	time to swim to shore.
80	Our lungs were changing. Soon we would only be able
90	to breathe air. 93

Comprehension Check

1. What happens to a crab when it molts? **Description**

2. Where will Hermie live after his lungs change? **Draw Conclusions**

	Words Read	–	Number of Errors	=	Words Correct Score
First Read		–		=	
Second Read		–		=	

© Macmillan/McGraw-Hill

At Home: Help your child read the passage, paying attention to the goal at the top of the page.

Synonyms are words that have the same or almost the same meaning.

Use the dictionary and thesaurus entries to answer the questions. Then circle the source you used.

Dictionary	Thesaurus
trash (trash) *noun* something you throw away **trip** (trip) I. *noun* to go from one place to another. 2. *verb* you hit your foot on something and almost fall	**trash** *noun* garbage, junk, rubbish **trip** *noun* drive, ride, journey *verb* fall, slip, stumble

I. What does **trash** mean? _____

dictionary   thesaurus

2. What is a synonym for the verb **trip**? _____

dictionary   thesaurus

3. What does the noun **trip** mean? _____

dictionary   thesaurus

4. What are two synonyms for **trash**? _____

dictionary   thesaurus

At Home: Help your child use the synonyms for *trash* and *trip* in sentences.

Name _____

Write the letters *i, igh, ie,* or *y* to complete each word.

1. Yesterday the sk_____ was cloudy and gray.

2. The stars did not come out last n_____t.

3. Our cat was not home b_____ eight o'clock.

4. She likes to l_____ under the front porch.

5. I knew that is where I would f_____nd her.

A **contraction** is a short way to write two words.

she is = **she's**   he is = **he's**

we are = **we're**   they are = **they're**

do not = **don't**   does not = **doesn't**

Write the contraction that takes the place of the words in dark print.

6. **She is** my sister, Lila. _____

7. **He is** my brother, Lou. _____

8. **We are** the first twins in our family. _____

9. Twins **do not** always look alike. _____

At Home: Have your child use each contraction in a
sentence of his or her own.

Captions are the words below a picture. They tell what the picture is about.

Match each caption to a picture. Write the letter in the box. Then write a different caption for each picture on the line below.

a. Go that way.   **b.** This is a painting.

c. We have fun.   **d.** This is a kitten.

I.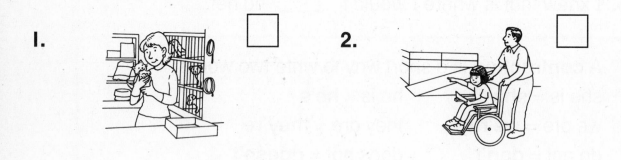

2.

_____   _____

_____   _____

3.

4.

_____   _____

_____   _____

 At Home: Have your child draw a picture. Then ask him or her to write a caption for it.

© Macmillan/McGraw-Hill

Name _____

Search for the words from the box. Circle each word as you find it. Then write it in the correct list below.

coach	no	slow	toe	ago
toad	glow	goat	bow	foe

```
I   T   O   E   C   V   O   B   T
Y   J   P   T   H   C   P   X   O
A   G   O   S   K   O   E   B   A
U   G   W   L   J   A   N   O   D
E   L   Z   O   O   C   L   W   Z
O   O   X   W   R   H   C   M   J
F   W   P   D   A   G   O   A   T
```

1. words with the long *o* sound as in *so*

_____

2. words with the long *o* sound as in *Joe*

_____

3. words with the long *o* sound as in *road*

_____

4. words with the long *o* sound as in *grow*

_____

At Home: Say a long *o* word and have your child say others that rhyme with it.

There's Nothing Like Baseball
Book 2.1/Unit 2

Choose a word from the box to match the group of clues that best describe its meaning.

uniform	coach	starting
tryouts	practices	imaginary

1. This word means events where people show their skills to gain

   a place on a team or in a play. _____

2. This is a word for a person who helps others improve their skills.

   _____

3. This is a word for events where people do the same skills over

   and over to try to get better at them. _____

4. This word describes pictures or ideas that a person might make
   up in his or her mind. It describes things you can't actually

   touch. _____

5. This word can mean a type of clothing worn by people on the

   same team or who do the same job. _____

6. Players who get to play first in a game are described by this

   word. _____

© Macmillan/McGraw-Hill

At Home: Help your child make up sentences for each of the vocabulary words above.

Name _____

As you read *There's Nothing Like Baseball*, fill in the Inference Chart.

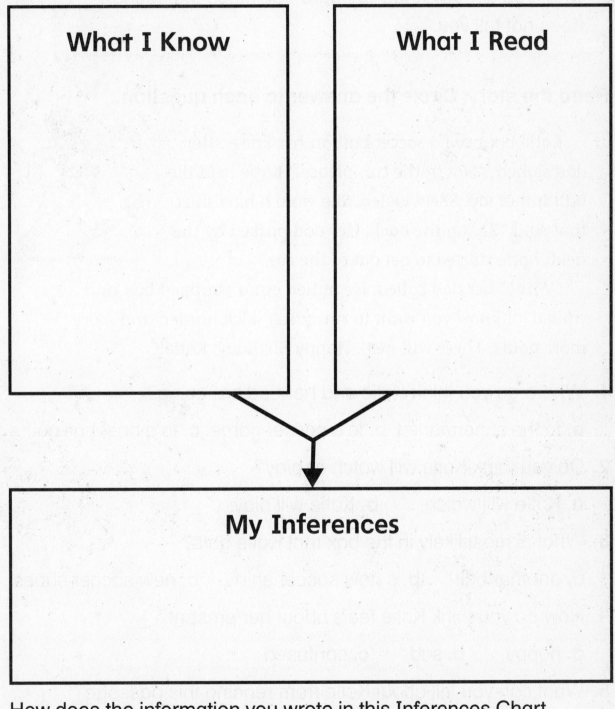

What I Know	What I Read

My Inferences

How does the information you wrote in this Inferences Chart help you to better understand *There's Nothing Like Baseball*?

At Home: Have your child use the chart to retell the story.

There's Nothing Like Baseball
Book 2.1/Unit 2

77

© Macmillan/McGraw-Hill

When you **make inferences**, you use story clues and what you already know to figure out things that the text does not tell you.

Read the story. Circle the answer to each question.

Katie bounced a soccer ball on her knees. Her dad sighed. "Not in the car, please." Katie held the ball in her lap. She wiggled. She wore a blue shirt that said "21" on the back. Her dad parked by the field. Katie started to get out of the car.

"Wait!" her dad called. He pulled out a wrapped box and smiled. "I know you want to run faster, kick harder, and score more goals. These will help. Happy Birthday, Katie!"

1. Where do you think Katie and her dad are going?

   a. to the supermarket **b.** to a soccer game **c.** to a baseball game

2. Do you think Katie will watch or play?

   a. Katie will watch.   **b.** Katie will play.

3. What is most likely in the box that Katie gets?

   a. another ball   **b.** a new soccer shirt   **c.** new soccer shoes

4. How do you think Katie feels about her present?

   a. happy   **b.** sad   **c.** confused

5. What can you tell about Katie from reading this passage?

   a. She likes soccer.   **b.** She likes ice cream.   **c.** She likes cats.

At Home: Encourage your child to make inferences based on facial expressions and gestures he or she sees in pictures or on television.

Name _____

As I read, I will pay attention to punctuation and expression.

	Harry woke up. He rolled over and **groaned**.
8	Getting up early was the worst part of training for
18	team **tryouts**. Starting last week, he'd been jogging
26	every morning. He wanted to be a strong runner,
35	just like his mom.
39	After school, Harry met his dad at the basketball
48	courts. Harry's dad was a great basketball player.
56	Harry was training for the basketball team as well
65	as the track team!
69	The night before the tryouts, Harry went to bed
78	early. He stared at his **uniform**. He wondered if he
88	could ever be a track star. What if he could become
99	a basketball superstar, too? 103

Comprehension Check

1. Why does Harry wonder if he could be a track or basketball star? **Make Inferences**

2. What is the sequence of events in Harry's day? **Sequence**

	Words Read	–	Number of Errors	=	Words Correct Score
First Read		–		=	
Second Read		–		=	

© Macmillan/McGraw-Hill

At Home: Help your child read the passage, paying attention to the goal at the top of the page.

Name _____

> **Multiple-meaning words** are words that have more
> than one meaning.

**Use the dictionary entry to figure out which meaning is
used in each sentence. Write the number of the meaning
that matches its use in the sentence.**

> **fall** *verb* **1.** to come down from a place. *Rain drops* **fall** *from
> the sky.* *noun* **2.** when something or someone comes
> down suddenly to the floor or ground. *Henry had a bad* **fall**
> *from his bicycle.* **3.** a season of the year. ***Fall*** *comes after
> summer and before winter.*

1. I will take gymnastics in the **fall.** _____

2. If we win this game, we will not **fall** from first place. _____

3. I was not hurt by the **fall.** _____

4. I am always careful not to **fall** off the diving board. _____

5. September is in the **fall.** _____

6. Dana was walking on the ice and had a **fall.** _____

 At Home: Encourage your child to compare the sentence in
a dictionary definition to the one he or she is reading to help
find the right meaning.

© Macmillan/McGraw-Hill

Name _____

> A **contraction** is a short way of writing two words. An apostrophe is used to take the place of the letters that are left out.
>
> we will = we'll   I have = I've

Replace the underlined words in each sentence with the correct contraction. Write the contraction on the line. Then circle all the words in each sentence that have the long *o* sound.

1. <u>I have</u> never been on a boat. _____

2. <u>We will</u> go to the park to play baseball. _____

3. <u>We have</u> never played with snow on the field.

   _____

4. Moe has a game that <u>you will</u> love. _____

5. <u>They have</u> had no practice this week. _____

6. <u>I will</u> bring the snacks, and Joan will bring the drinks.

   _____

7. <u>They will</u> sit in the first row. _____

8. <u>You have</u> never played soccer with Joe. _____

At Home: Look through a book or magazine and have your child find five words that have the long *o* sound.

There's Nothing Like Baseball
Book 2.1/Unit 2 81

© Macmillan/McGraw-Hill

Newspapers and magazines often use **bar graphs** to compare amounts.

Read the graph. Circle the correct answer to each question.

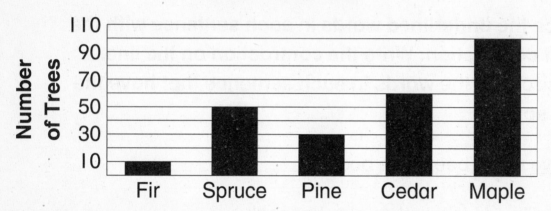

Trees in Pineville

1. What is being compared?

　a. height of trees　　**b.** number of trees

2. Which kind of tree is least common in Pineville?

　a. fir　　**b.** maple

3. Which kind of tree is most common in Pineville?

　a. fir　　**b.** maple

4. The state tree is the pine. Pineville wants to have more pines than any other tree. Does the town need to plant more pines?

　a. Yes　　**b.** No

5. How many spruce trees are in Pineville?

　a. 10　　**b.** 50　　**c.** 60　　**d.** 100

© Macmillan/McGraw-Hill

At Home: Have your child look through a newspaper or a magazine and point out to you all the graphs he or she finds.

A. Use words from the box to complete the paragraph.

coach	stay	personal	starting	recognized

We _____ after school to watch baseball

practice. We watch the _____ and the players. Each

player hits, catches, and runs bases. The _____

players are the ones who play first in a game. On Monday the top

pitcher _____ us. He waved. We waved back. We

are his _____ fan club.

B. Use words from the box to complete the crossword puzzle.

hunger	desert	road	informs	tryouts

Across

4. what you feel when you need to eat

5. an area that is hot and dry

Down

1. tells someone about something

2. tests to get on a team or in a
   performance group

3. street or path

© Macmillan/McGraw-Hill

Name _____

A. Match each word to its meaning. Then write the letter next to the word on the line.

1. neighbor _____   **a.** saved

2. rescued _____   **b.** in pieces

3. broken _____   **c.** a solid shape like a block

4. vanished _____   **d.** looked closely

5. peered _____   **e.** someone living nearby

6. cube _____   **f.** disappeared

B. Write the word from the box that completes each sentence.

| flight | drove | gently | examines |

1. The breeze _____ rocked the hammock.

2. We watched the _____ of the eagles high in the sky.

3. Mom _____ us home after school.

4. My doctor _____ me carefully when I have a checkup.

Name _____

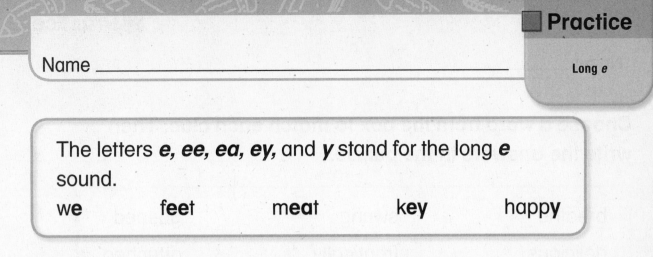

The letters **e, ee, ea, ey,** and **y** stand for the long **e** sound.

w**e**   f**ee**t   m**ea**t   **key**   happ**y**

Write the missing letter or letters to complete each word.

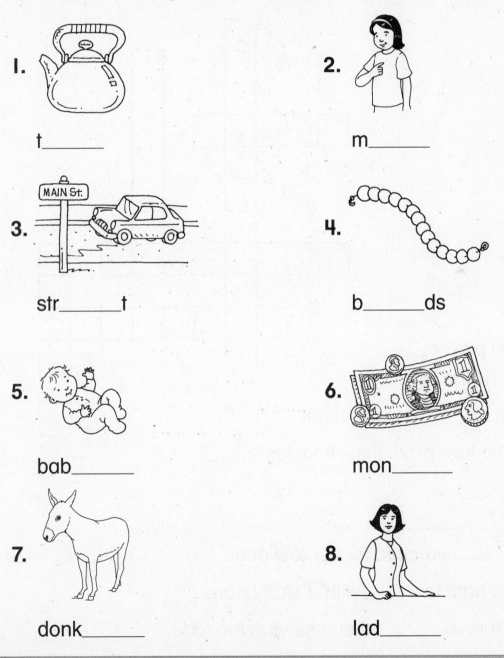

1. t_____

2. m_____

3. str_____t

4. b_____ds

5. bab_____

6. mon_____

7. donk_____

8. lad_____

 At Home: Help your child suggest other words that have *e,* *ee, ea, ey,* or *y* that make the long *e* sound. Have him or her use each word in a sentence.

Head, Body, Legs • **Book 2.1/Unit 3** 85

Name _____

Choose a word from the box to match each clue. Then write the answers in the puzzle.

breathe	swung	gasped
delicious	frantically	attached

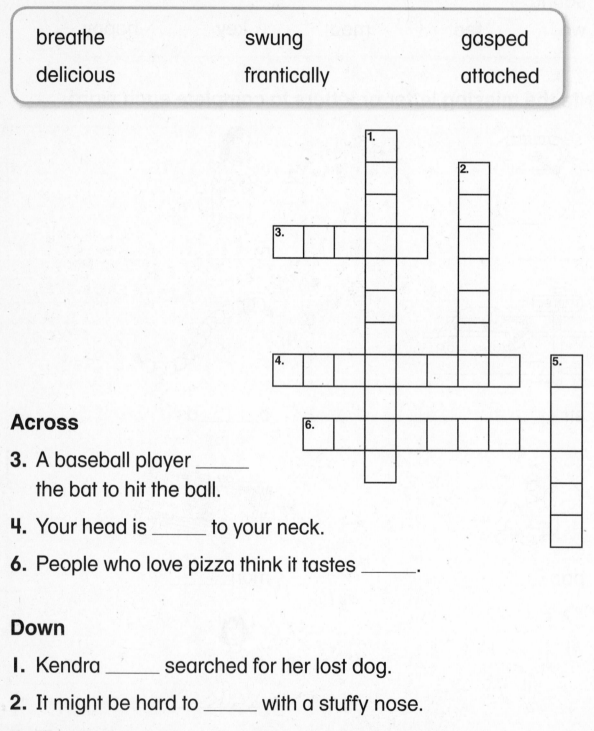

Across

3. A baseball player _____ the bat to hit the ball.

4. Your head is _____ to your neck.

6. People who love pizza think it tastes _____.

Down

1. Kendra _____ searched for her lost dog.

2. It might be hard to _____ with a stuffy nose.

5. The tired runner _____ when she won the race.

Name _____

As you read *Head, Body, Legs: A Story from Liberia,* **fill in the Cause and Effect Chart.**

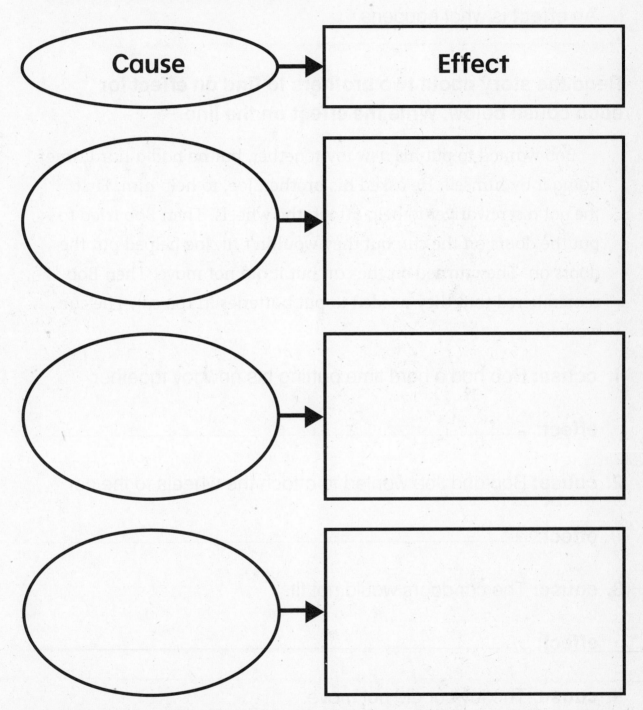

How does the information you wrote in this Cause and Effect Chart help you to better understand *Head, Body, Legs: A Story from Liberia*?

At Home: Have your child use the chart to retell the story.

A **cause** is the reason something happens.

An **effect** is what happens.

Read the story about two brothers to find an effect for each cause below. Write the effect on the line.

Bob wanted to put his new toy together, but he had a hard time doing it by himself. He asked his brother, Joe, to help him. First Joe got a screwdriver to help attach the wheels. Then Bob tried to put the doors on the car, but they wouldn't fit. Joe helped put the doors on. They turned on the car, but it did not move. Then Bob remembered that they needed to put batteries in the car. The car worked!

1. **cause:** Bob had a hard time putting his new toy together.

    effect: _____

2. **cause:** Bob and Joe wanted to attach the wheels to the car.

    effect: _____

3. **cause:** The car doors would not fit.

    effect: _____

4. **cause:** The toy car did not move.

    effect: _____

At Home: Have your child read a storybook and look for examples of cause and effect.

As I read, I will pay attention to the punctuation in each sentence.

	A fisherman lived with his wife in a little house.
10	Every morning he went to the sea. He tried to catch
21	fish to eat.
24	One day the fisherman caught nothing. Then he
32	felt a strong tug on his fishing line. The fishing rod
43	swung from side to side. The fisherman fought
51	**frantically** to hold on to it.
57	The fisherman reeled in the line. There
64	was a golden fish **attached** to his hook.
72	"Please let me go!" it cried. "I cannot **breathe** out
82	of water!"
84	The fish was beautiful. But it was too small to
94	eat, so the fisherman let it go. 101

Comprehension Check

1. What made the fisherman's fishing rod swing from side to side?
Draw Conclusions

2. Why did the fisherman go down to the sea every morning?
Cause and Effect

	Words Read	–	Number of Errors	=	Words Correct Score
First Read		–		=	
Second Read		–		=	

© Macmillan/McGraw-Hill

At Home: Help your child read the passage, paying attention to the goal at the top of the page.

Head, Body, Legs • Book 2.1/Unit 3   **89**

Sometimes the other words in a sentence can help you figure out the meaning of a new word. These words are **context clues** and can come before or after an unknown word.

Read each sentence. Then circle the meaning of the word in dark type.

1. The teacher let Lorna and me work on the project **together**, so each of us completed half of the work.

   with another person   alone

2. The **coach** helps us learn to throw and hit balls.

   person who trains a team   a type of ball

3. Each camper completed a **task** to help the camp.

   camp   job

4. Everyone got along and **cooperated** to get the job done.

   worked together   worked separately

5. Megan used a screwdriver to **assemble** the toy house.

   play with   build

6. All of us **participated** in the reading program by reading five books each.

   took part   ate

At Home: Help your child identify four new words that describe something in his or her home. Then have your child write a sentence that gives a clue to each word's meaning.

A word part that is added to the end of a word to change its meaning is called a **suffix**.

The suffix **-less** means "without."

The suffix **-ful** means "full of."

When you add **-ful** or **-less** to a word that ends with **y**, you drop the **y** and add **i** before adding the suffix.

mercy + ful = merc**i**ful

Write a word that means the same as the group of words. Your new word will end in *-less* or *-ful* and have a long *e* sound.

1. full of beauty

_____

2. without need

_____

3. without sleep

_____

4. full of meaning

_____

5. full of peace

_____

6. without seeds

_____

7. without a penny

_____

8. full of glee

_____

© Macmillan/McGraw-Hill

At Home: Have your child add *-ful* and *-less* to five words and write a sentence for each word.

Name _____

A home page on the Internet is the starting place for getting information. It has links to other related information on the Web site. A **drop-down menu** will help you find more links.

Look at the home page below. Then follow the directions and answer the question.

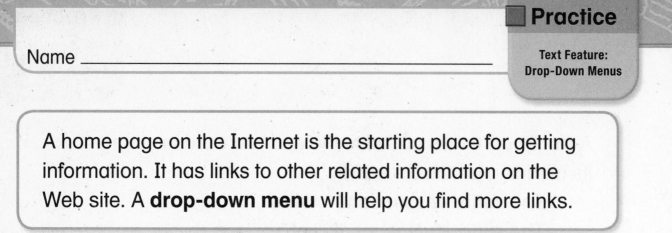

1. What is the title of this Web page?

_____

2. What are two links under products?

_____

3. Where would you find the link Summer Camp?

_____

4. What would you click on to contact the president of Stories Galore?

_____

At Home: Ask your child to name other things that might be found in a drop-down menu.

Name _____

> Listen to the long **u** sound as you say each of these words.
>
> **mule**   **use**   **tune**

A. Choose the word from the box that names each picture. Careful! You will not use all the words in the box.

> | rug | tuba | June | use |
> |-----|------|------|-----|
> | cube | cub | cute | mule |

1. _____

2. _____

3. _____

4. _____

B. Find the words from the box with the long *u* sound that do not name a picture. Then write a sentence for each word on the lines below.

5. _____

6. _____

At Home: Ask your child to tell you two words that have the long *u* sound.

Officer Buckle and Gloria
Book 2.1/Unit 3

93

Name _____

A. Read the passage. Choose a word from the box to complete each sentence. Write it on the line.

tips   obeys   accident   buddy   enormous   attention

Our class took a field trip to the zoo. I couldn't believe how big

the zoo was. It was _____! Each of us had to hold

hands with a _____. We paid _____
to our teacher. He told us the rules. He said, "A good student

_____ the rules. Following rules can keep you

from having an _____. I don't want you to get
hurt or lost." Our teacher also gave us good ideas about what to

look for at the zoo. His _____ helped us have a
good time.

B. Use two vocabulary words to write two new sentences.

1. _____

2. _____

Name _____

As you read *Officer Buckle and Gloria,* fill in the
Illustrations Chart.

Illustration	What I Learn From the Picture

How does the information you wrote in this Illustrations Chart help
you to better understand *Officer Buckle and Gloria*?

At Home: Have your child use the chart to retell the story.

Officer Buckle and Gloria
Book 2.1/Unit 3

95

© Macmillan/McGraw-Hill

Name _____

Illustrations are pictures that go with a story or article. They can help you understand what you are reading.

Look at each illustration and read the sentence. Use the illustration to help you answer the question. Then fill in the circle in front of the correct answer.

1. The girl wore her safety gear when she skated.
   Which is part of <u>safety gear</u>?
   (a) window
   (b) helmet
   (c) dog

2. The boy put on his life jacket so he could go on the boat.
   Which letter shows the <u>life jacket</u>?
   (a) a
   (b) b
   (c) c

3. We stayed on the curb because the bus was approaching.
   An approaching school bus is _____.
   (a) leaving
   (b) coming
   (c) stopped

4. We were careful to keep our hands away from the porcupine.
   What is a <u>porcupine</u>?
   (a) a drink
   (b) a hat
   (c) an animal

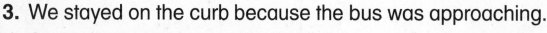

© Macmillan/McGraw-Hill

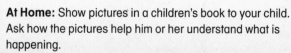

At Home: Show pictures in a children's book to your child. Ask how the pictures help him or her understand what is happening.

Name _____

As I read, I will pay attention to the punctuation in each sentence.

	Roads can be dangerous places. Pay attention when you
9	are on or near a road. If you are not careful, an accident
22	may happen. Here are some tips to keep you safe.
32	Always walk on the sidewalk. If there is no sidewalk,
42	walk on the side of the road. Face cars coming toward you.
54	You should also be careful when crossing the road.
63	A safe pedestrian obeys these rules.
69	Follow these five steps when you need to cross the road:
80	**Step 1: STOP** at the side of the road.
88	**Step 2: LOOK** for any traffic.
93	**Step 3: LISTEN** for any traffic that might be coming.
102	**Step 4: WAIT** until there is no traffic before you cross.
112	**Step 5: GO** when it is safe to cross. 120

Comprehension Check

1. Why should you pay attention when you are on or near a road?
Main Idea and Details

2. Why do you think it is a good idea to wait until there is no traffic to cross the street? **Make Inferences**

	Words Read	–	Number of Errors	=	Words Correct Score
First Read		–		=	
Second Read		–		=	

At Home: Help your child read the passage, paying attention to the goal at the top of the page.

Officer Buckle and Gloria
Book 2.1/Unit 3

97

> **Synonyms** are words that have the same or almost the same meaning.

Read each pair of sentences. A word in the first sentence and a word in the second sentence are synonyms. Circle the synonyms. Then write them on the lines.

1. It was time for Gina to go.

   She was ready to leave.

   _____ _____

2. Gina put on her helmet to begin her bike ride.

   She could not wait to start.

   _____ _____

3. Gina had to ride her mom's big bike.

   The large bike was a little bit hard to ride.

   _____ _____

4. Gina was careful as she rode quickly.

   She wanted to get to her friend's house fast.

   _____ _____

© Macmillan/McGraw-Hill

At Home: Ask your child to tell you a synonym for each of these words: *yell, near, correct.*

Name _____

Say these words and listen to the long *u* sound.

cute   **duke**

A. Answer each riddle with a word from the box. Careful! You will not use all the words in the box.

mud	hug	tube	tub	tune
cub	mule	sun	menu	bush

I. You can sing and play me. What am I? _____

2. I can be stubborn. I look like a horse. What am I?

_____

3. You look at me to choose what to eat. What am I? _____

4. Toothpaste comes inside of me. What am I? _____

B. Choose two words from the box that have the long *u* sound. Write a sentence for each word on the lines.

5. _____

6. _____

At Home: Ask your child to tell you two words that have the long *u* sound and to use each one in a sentence.

Officer Buckle and Gloria
Book 2.1/Unit 3

 99

© Macmillan/McGraw-Hill

Name _____

> A **floor plan** is a small map of a building. It shows where you
> can find rooms and other things in a building.

Read the floor plan. Then circle the correct answer to complete each sentence.

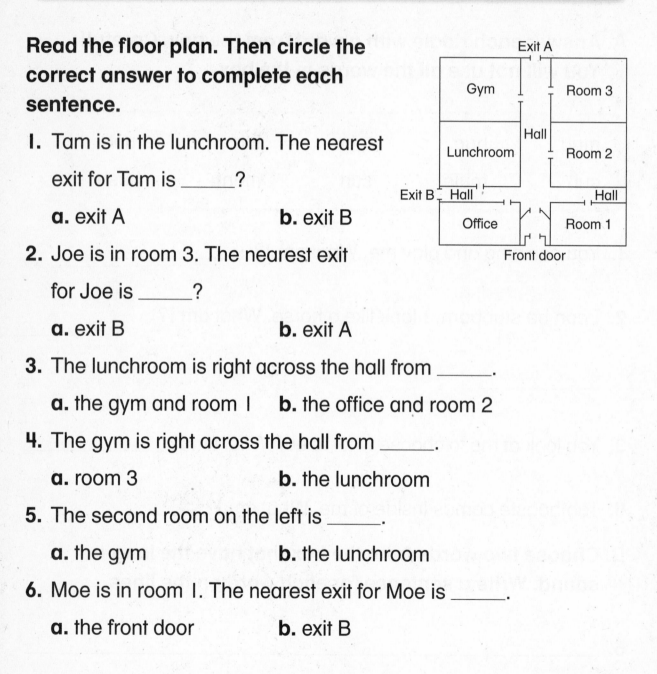

1. Tam is in the lunchroom. The nearest exit for Tam is _____?

   a. exit A   **b.** exit B

2. Joe is in room 3. The nearest exit for Joe is _____?

   a. exit B   **b.** exit A

3. The lunchroom is right across the hall from _____.

   a. the gym and room 1   **b.** the office and room 2

4. The gym is right across the hall from _____.

   a. room 3   **b.** the lunchroom

5. The second room on the left is _____.

   a. the gym   **b.** the lunchroom

6. Moe is in room 1. The nearest exit for Moe is _____.

   a. the front door   **b.** exit B

© Macmillan/McGraw-Hill

 At Home: Help your child draw a floor plan of your home and label each room.

Name _____

A **consonant digraph** is two consonants that together stand for only one sound. Say these words. Then listen for the sounds made by the letters in dark print.

thin   **sh**ed   **wh**en   **ch**op

Choose the group of letters from the box that completes each word. Write the letters on the line.

th   sh   wh   ch

1. I took a walk _____rough the park.

2. There was a _____ill in the wintry air.

3. I _____all find a fossil, I thought.

4. I looked for a long time but did not see a _____ing.

5. Then I saw a flat _____ite piece of rock with a pattern on it.

6. The pattern on the rock was in the _____ape of a leaf.

7. _____en I saw the leaf, I knew I was lucky.

8. My rock _____ip was a fossil!

 **At Home:** Have your child make up and say aloud new sentences for the words he or she wrote.

Name _____

A. Write words from the box to complete the story.

hopeful	unable	confirm	ancient	valid

Sasha found a little bone in her yard. The bone was covered in dirt as if it had been there for many years. It looked

_____. Maybe it was a dinosaur bone! Sasha was

excited and _____ about this idea.

"Let's try to _____ what it is," Dad said. They looked at pictures in dinosaur books. They tried and tried but

were _____ to find a bone that looked like the one Sasha had found. Sasha still thought it was a dinosaur bone. Dad

said, "Your idea might be _____. Or maybe you found a chicken bone from a picnic last summer!"

B. Use a word from the box to add another sentence to the story.

_____

_____

As you read _Meet the Super Croc_, fill in the Summary Chart.

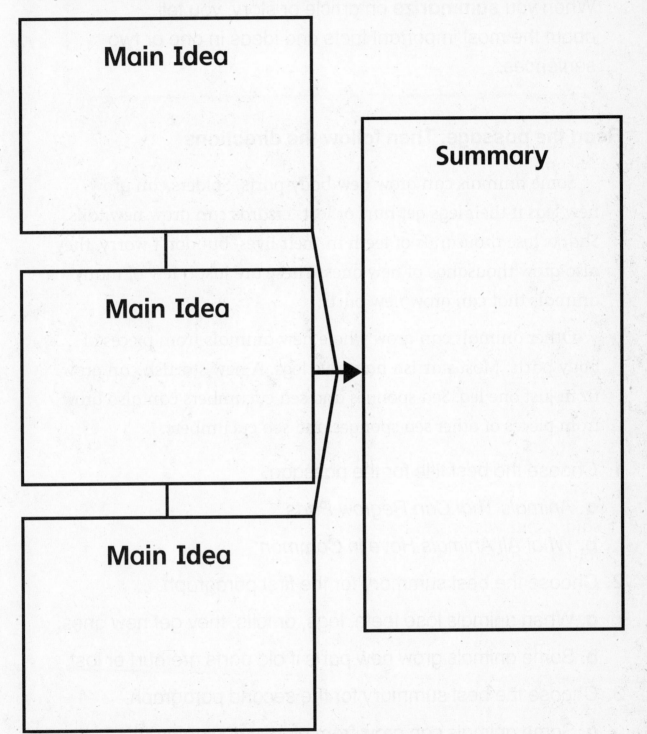

Main Idea

Main Idea

Main Idea

Summary

How does the information you wrote in this Summarize Chart help you to better understand _Meet the Super Croc_?

At Home: Have your child use the chart to retell the story.

Meet the Super Croc
Book 2.1/Unit 3

103

© Macmillan/McGraw-Hill

Name _____

When you **summarize** an article or story, you tell about the most important facts and ideas in one or two sentences.

Read the passage. Then follow the directions.

Some animals can grow new body parts. Spiders can grow new legs if their legs get hurt or lost. Lizards can grow new tails. Sharks lose thousands of teeth in their lives, but don't worry, they also grow thousands of new ones. These are just a few of many animals that can grow new parts.

Other animals can grow whole new animals from pieces of body parts. Most starfish have five legs. A new starfish can grow from just one leg. Sea sponges and sea cucumbers can also grow from pieces of other sea sponges and sea cucumbers.

1. Choose the best title for the passage.

   a. *Animals That Can Regrow Parts*

   b. *What All Animals Have in Common*

2. Choose the best summary for the first paragraph.

   a. When animals lose teeth, legs, or tails, they get new ones.

   b. Some animals grow new parts if old parts are hurt or lost.

3. Choose the best summary for the second paragraph.

   a. Some animals can grow from pieces of an animal.

   b. There are animals called sea sponges and sea cucumbers.

© Macmillan/McGraw-Hill

 At Home: Have your child summarize his or her day at school in two or three sentences.

Name _____

Practice

Vocabulary Strategy:
Suffixes and Prefixes

A word part that is added to the end of a word to change its meaning is called a **suffix.** A word part that is added to the beginning of a word to change its meaning is called a **prefix.**

Suffixes

-ful = "full of"

-less = "without"

Prefixes

re- = "again"

un- = "not"

dis- = "do the opposite of"

Complete each sentence with a new word made from one of the base words and one of the prefixes or suffixes below. Use any word part more than once if you need to.

Prefixes:		Base words:		Suffixes:
re- un- dis-	**+**	use care visit like	**+**	-ful -less

I. A raccoon was at our campsite last night and it may

_____ us tonight.

2. This dinosaur book is very _____ to our class.

3. I _____ burned toast.

4. The peacock's tail is _____ any other bird's tail.

5. It was _____ of you to let the dog out.

© Macmillan/McGraw-Hill

At Home: Have your child put together different word parts from the box to create more words. Discuss how prefixes and suffixes change the meaning of the base word.

Name _____

Before you write a report, you need to choose a topic. You
need to **narrow the topic** until it is small enough to cover in
the space you have. Plan to focus on just one or two main
ideas so your topic is not too big.

A. Read the sentences below. Then answer the questions.

Liam has to research and write a one-page report about one
animal. He plans to write about mammals.

I. Is Liam's topic idea a good one for his report? Why or why not?

_____

_____

B. Write three examples of better topic ideas for Liam.

2. _____ 3. _____

4. _____

5. Tell why your ideas would work well for Liam's report.

_____

_____

_____

 At Home: Give your child the following made-up assignment: *Write
a one-page report about one sport.* Challenge your child to come up
with three topic ideas that would work well for this assignment.

As I read, I will pay attention to punctuation and the pronunciation of the vocabulary word.

	Have you ever seen a living dinosaur? Of course
9	not! Dinosaurs are extinct. They no longer exist.
17	All of the dinosaurs died out about 65 million years
26	ago. No one really knows why. Some scientists think
35	it was because Earth's climate changed.
41	Many other animals are also extinct. Some
48	became extinct in **ancient** times. Others became
55	extinct less than 100 years ago. Let's learn about
63	some of them.
66	The woolly mammoth looked like an elephant.
73	But woolly mammoths were even bigger!
79	Like elephants, woolly mammoths had tusks and a
87	trunk. Unlike elephants, they had long, shaggy hair
95	all over their bodies. Woolly mammoths lived during
103	the Ice Age. Their long hair kept them warm. 112

Comprehension Check

1. What does it mean for an animal to be extinct? **Summarize**

2. How were woolly mammoths like elephants? **Main Idea and Details**

	Words Read	−	Number of Errors	=	Words Correct Score
First Read		−		=	
Second Read		−		=	

© Macmillan/McGraw-Hill

At Home: Help your child read the passage, paying attention to the goal at the top of the page.

Meet the Super Croc

A **prefix** is a word part that can be added to the beginning of a word to change its meaning.

re- = "again"   *un-* = "not"   *dis-* = "opposite of"

Read each sentence. Choose the correct group of letters from the box to complete the word. Write the letters on the line. Then write the meaning of the underlined word on the line below.

wh	sh	ch	th

1. David will <u>redraw</u> the picture of the _____air.

_____

2. I will read the card _____ile you <u>unwrap</u> your present.

_____

3. Tara <u>disagreed</u> with Sam's _____ird answer.

_____

4. We have a _____ance to help <u>rejoin</u> the dinosaur

bones. _____

At Home: Work with your child to think of other words that have the prefixes *re-*, *un-*, or *dis-*. Discuss how the prefixes change the words' meanings.

© Macmillan/McGraw-Hill

Name _____

Write a word from the box to answer each clue.

leash	booth	graph	stitches
pitcher	mashed	mouth	teacher

1. You may sit here in a diner

   or restaurant. _____

2. Some people like their potatoes

   made this way. _____

3. Use this when walking the dog. _____

4. You can learn a lot from this person. _____

5. Fix a rip in your clothes with these. _____

6. You look at this for information. _____

7. You use this when you talk and eat. _____

8. This baseball player throws the ball to the batter.

   _____

At Home: Help your child say each word and listen for the sounds *th, sh, ch,* and *tch.* Ask him or her to suggest other words that have these sounds.

The Alvin Ailey Kids
Book 2.1/Unit 3   109

A. Write the word from the box to complete each sentence.

| remember | students | perform | effort | proud | mood |

I. Charlene's hard work and _____ really paid off.

2. The school band will _____ next week.

3. Ruthann was _____ to be singing in the school play.

4. Nathan can _____ his lines for the play.

5. Pizza for lunch always puts me in a good _____.

6. All the _____ and teachers like to sing.

B. Choose two words from the box. Write a sentence for each word on the lines below.

7. _____

8. _____

© Macmillan/McGraw-Hill

Name _____

As you read *The Alvin Ailey Kids: Dancing As a Team,*
fill in the Summarize Chart.

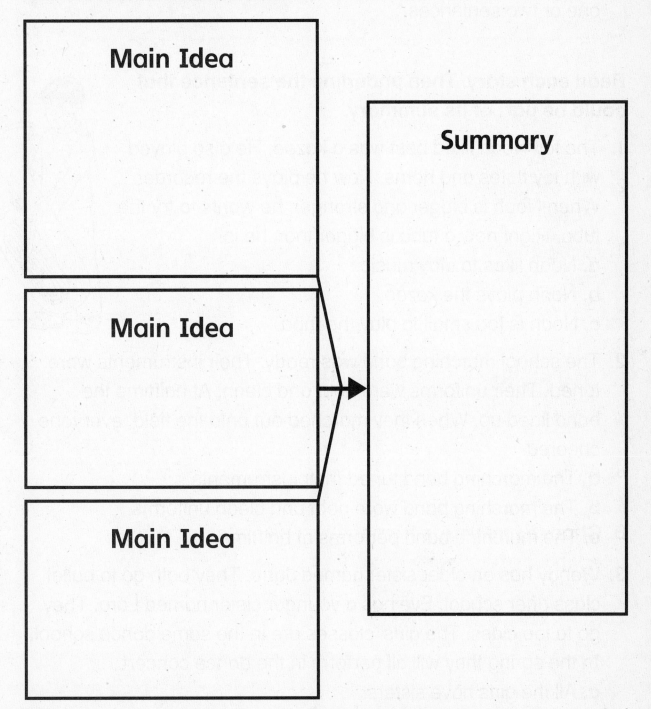

How does the information you wrote in this Summarize Chart help
you to better understand *The Alvin Ailey Kids: Dancing As a Team*?

At Home: Have your child use the chart to retell the story.

The Alvin Ailey Kids
Book 2.1/Unit 3

111

A **summary** tells what an article or story is about in just one or two sentences.

Read each story. Then underline the sentence that could be part of its summary.

1. The toy Noah liked best was a kazoo. He also played with toy flutes and horns. Now he plays the recorder. When Noah is bigger and stronger, he wants to try the tuba. Right now a tuba is bigger than he is!
   a. Noah likes to play music.
   b. Noah plays the kazoo.
   c. Noah is too small to play the tuba.

2. The school marching band was ready. Their instruments were tuned. Their uniforms were neat and clean. At halftime the band lined up. When they marched out onto the field, everyone cheered.
   a. The marching band tuned their instruments.
   b. The marching band wore neat and clean uniforms.
   c. The marching band performs at halftime.

3. Wendy has an older sister named Jane. They both go to ballet class after school. Eve has a younger sister named Lara. They go to tap class. The girls' classes are in the same dance school. In the spring they will all perform in the dance concert.
   a. All the girls have sisters.
   b. All the girls like to dance.
   c. The dance concert is in the spring.

© Macmillan/McGraw-Hill

At Home: Have your child summarize his or her day at school or an afternoon activity in one or two sentences.

Name _____

As I read, I will pay attention to the punctuation.

	When Nan was eight, she joined a sports school
9	in the Chinese city of Beijing (bay-JING). Only the
17	best child athletes in the country live and train at
27	special schools like this one.
32	Training to be a gymnast is hard work. Children
41	begin with stretches at 6:30 in the morning! Next,
49	they go into classrooms. That is where they are
58	taught reading, math, and other lessons until
65	lunchtime. There is a lot to **remember**.
72	After lunch, the younger **students** take a nap.
80	Then training goes on until dinnertime. Sometimes
87	the children **perform** the same exercise for an hour.
96	They only stop when they do it right. 104

Comprehension Check

1. What did Nan do when she was eight? **Main Idea and Details**

2. When does the training day begin at Nan's school? **Main Idea and Details**

	Words Read	–	Number of Errors	=	Words Correct Score
First Read		–		=	
Second Read		–		=	

At Home: Help your child read the passage, paying attention to the goal at the top of the page.

The Alvin Ailey Kids
Book 2.1/Unit 3   113

© Macmillan/McGraw-Hill

Look for the definition of words in the **dictionary**.
Use a **thesaurus** to find antonyms and synonyms.

Dictionary	Thesaurus	
applaud (uh-**plawd**) *verb* To show that you like something by clapping your hands.	**applaud**	*synonyms*: clap, appreciate *antonyms*: boo, hiss, jeer
chorus (**kor**-uhss) *noun* A group of people who sing or dance together.	**chorus**	*synonyms*: choir, glee club *antonyms*: star, soloist

Read each sentence. Use the dictionary and thesaurus entries above to find an antonym for the word in dark print. Then write the new word on the line.

I. We were excited to see the show. We began to **boo** as the

performers came on stage. _____

2. The **soloist** stood along the back of the stage.

_____

3. The **chorus** stood at the front of the stage. _____

4. When the beautiful song ended, we did not hear anyone

applaud. _____

© Macmillan/McGraw-Hill

At Home: Ask your child to tell about a show or movie he or she saw. Write down what he or she says. Help your child suggest synonyms and antonyms for some of those words.

Name _____

> Listen to the sounds made by the letters **ch, sh, ph, tch,** and **th.**
>
> teach   wish   orphan   watch   tooth

Circle the word in ( ) that best completes each sentence.

I. In the summer my family goes to the (bead/beach) a lot.

2. Dad (washes/walks) the car when it is dirty.

3. I give my baby brother a (bath/back) each night.

4. I want to (teach/reach) when I grow up.

5. I need to make a (shone/phone) call.

> An **open syllable** ends with a vowel. The vowel sound is often long.
>
> broken = **bro/ken**
>
> A **closed syllable** ends with a consonant. The vowel sound is often short.
>
> picnic = **pic/nic**

Say each word. Draw a line between the syllables. Then circle *open* or *closed* to tell about the first syllable in each word.

5. music   open   closed

6. bottle   open   closed

7. label   open   closed

8. picture   open   closed

© Macmillan/McGraw-Hill

At Home: Have your child find one or more examples of words with open and closed syllables in a book he or she is reading.

> **Alliteration** is the repeated use of the same beginning sound in a group of words.
>
>   **A**lice sells **a**pples in **A**tlanta.
>
> **Rhythmic patterns** are sounds and words that repeat to make a rhythm.
>
>   Mary had a little lamb, little lamb, little lamb.

Read the lyrics to this American folk song. Then follow the directions.

Sunny valley, sunny valley,

Sunny valley low.

When you're in that sunny valley,

Sing it soft and slow.

Stormy ocean, stormy ocean,

Stormy ocean wide.

When you're on that stormy ocean,

There's no place you can hide.

1. Circle the group of words in these lyrics that show alliteration.

2. Underline two groups of words in these lyrics that repeat to give a certain rhythm.

© Macmillan/McGraw-Hill

 At Home: Help your child write a sentence that shows alliteration.

Name _____

Some words begin with three consonants. The words
street, scrub, and *spray* all begin with three consonant
sounds. Blend the consonant sounds together so that
each sound is heard.

s t r eet   **s c r** ub   **s p r** ay

**Read the name of each picture. Find words from the box that
begin with the same sounds. Write the words on the lines.**

scream	sprain	scrape	stream	scrub	spray
string	splint	street	strict	screen	strap

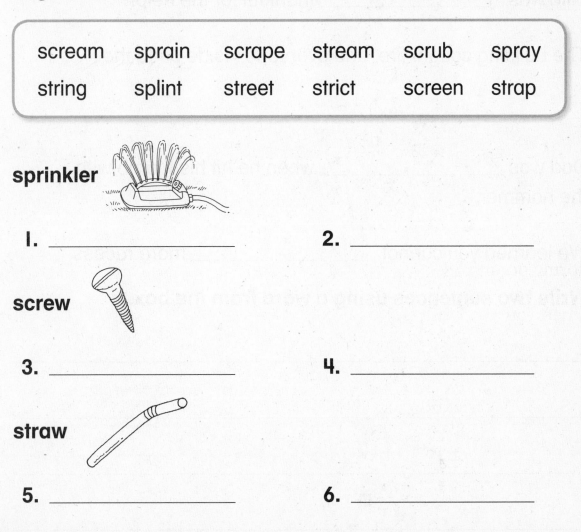

sprinkler

1. _____   2. _____

screw

3. _____   4. _____

straw

5. _____   6. _____

At Home: Write words that start with *scr, str,* and *spr* and
have your child sort them by initial consonant blend.

Click, Clack, Moo: Cows
That Type • **Book 2.1/Unit 3**

A. Choose a word from the box to finish each sentence.
Then write the word on the line.

| furious snoop emergency impatient demand sincerely |

1. Max felt _____ as he waited in line.

2. Ben knew not to _____ through the wrapped gifts.

3. Milo was _____ thankful for the help.

4. The building caught fire, and everyone inside used the

_____ exit.

5. Dad was _____ when he hit his thumb with
the hammer.

6. We learned you cannot _____ more recess.

B. Write two sentences using a word from the box.

7. _____

_____

8. _____

_____

As you read *Click, Clack, Moo: Cows That Type,* **fill in the Cause and Effect Chart.**

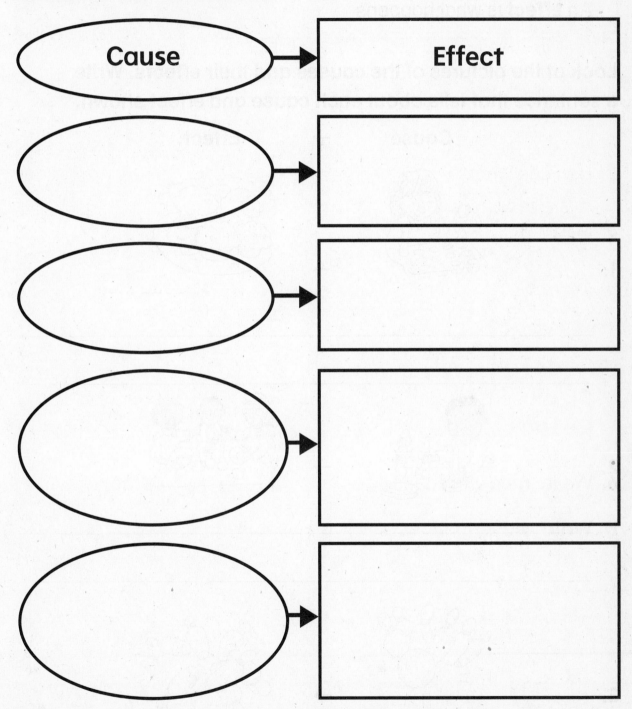

Cause

Effect

How does the information you wrote in this Cause and Effect Chart help you to better understand *Click, Clack, Moo: Cows That Type?*

 At Home: Have your child use the chart to retell the story.

Click, Clack, Moo: Cows
That Type • **Book 2.1/Unit 3**

119

The reason why or how something happens is the **cause**.
An **effect** is what happens.

**Look at the pictures of the causes and their effects. Write
a sentence that tells about each cause and effect shown.**

Cause → Effect

1.  →

_____

2.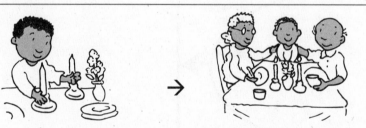

_____

_____

3.  →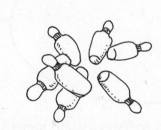

_____

Click, Clack, Moo: Cows
That Type • **Book 2.1/Unit 3**

 At Home: As you read a story with your child, ask him or her
to point out the cause and effect relationships in the story.

As I read, I will pay attention to tempo and copy tone and expression when reading words that have special type.

	Next door was Farmer Rosie's farm. Farmer Rosie's sheep
9	were watching.
11	"What's going on next door?" they asked. "Selina, **snoop**
20	for us!"
22	Selina his behind a fence post.
28	"They're knitting!" said Selina. "You hold two sticks and
37	some wool. Then you say a rhyme. *Knit and knit. Knit. Knitwit.*
49	*Make a sweater that will fit!"*
55	Now Farmer Rosie's sheep had Knitting Fever, too!
63	Then Selina had an idea. "Let's see who can knit the most
75	sweaters!" she shouted. "Our team will be the Woolly Sweaters."
85	"And our team will be the Knitwits," said Sharon.
94	"This is our rhyme," said Selina. *"You are good, but we are*
106	*better. You can't beat a Woolly Sweater!"* 113

Comprehension Check

1. Why do Farmer Rosie's sheep get Knitting Fever? **Cause and Effect**

2. What happens after Farmer Rosie's sheep get Knitting Fever? **Sequence**

	Words Read	−	Number of Errors	=	Words Correct Score
First Read		−		=	
Second Read		−		=	

At Home: Help your child read the passage, paying attention to the goal at the top of the page.

Name _____

Synonyms are words that have almost the same meaning.
You can use a thesaurus to find synonyms for many words.

Cap and *lid* are synonyms.

I put the **cap** on the bottle.   I put the **lid** on the bottle.

**Replace *big* in each sentence with a synonym that
makes sense. Write the new sentence on the line.**

   big *adjective* I. Large in size: *The elephant is a **big** animal.*
large, gigantic, huge 2. Of great importance: *Our trip to Florida is
a **big** event for us.* **important, major, notable 3.** Grown-up: *When
I'm **big**, I'll be a doctor.* **adult, older, mature**

I. I am going to travel when I am big.

_____

2. It was a small wedding but a big event.

_____

3. Our yard is *big* so it takes a long time to mow it.

_____

4. We practiced hard for the *big* game.

_____

At Home: Help your child find a word he or she already
knows well. Then help him or her find at least two synonyms
for that word.

Name _____

A **possessive** noun tells who or what owns something.
Add an **apostrophe (')** and **s** to a singular noun to
make it possessive.

**Write the possessive that can take the place of the
underlined words. Then choose a consonant blend from
the box to complete each word in dark print.**

str-	scr-	spr-

1. <u>The cat that belongs to Mia</u> loves his _____**atching**

   post. _____

2. <u>The crayons that belong to Mark</u> are _____**ead** all over

   the table. _____

3. <u>The arms that belong to Dad</u> are _____**onger** than

   mine. _____

4. <u>The shirt that belongs to Clint</u> has many _____**ipes**.

   _____

5. Mom used <u>the tools that belong to Sarah</u> to _____**ape**

   the ice away. _____

At Home: Have your child practice writing possessives
using the names of people and objects in your home.

Name _____

> **Calendars** show the days, weeks, and months in a year.

Read the calendar. Then write the answer for each question.

December						
S	M	T	W	T	F	S
			1	2	3	4
5	6	7	8	9	10	11
12	13	14	15	16	17	
19	20	21	22	23	24	25
26	27	28	29	30	31	

1. How many days are in the month?

_____

2. On which day of the week will the next month begin?

_____

3. How many Fridays are in this month? _____

4. Is that more, less, or the same as the number of Saturdays?

_____

5. If today is the 8th and something exciting is happening on the 20th, how many more days do you have to wait?

_____

6. What day of the week is the 20th? _____

7. Which symbol on the calendar shows a birthday party?

_____

8. On which day and date is the birthday party?

_____

© Macmillan/McGraw-Hill

At Home: Help your child read the calendars in your home. Have him or her find today's date and the dates of any upcoming events, such as parties or holidays.

Name _____

A. Write the word from the box that means the same or almost the same as the underlined word or words in each sentence.

| music | remember | attached | confirm | springs |

1. My hood is <u>connected</u> to my coat. _____

2. I <u>recall</u> the way to Art's house! _____

3. Mom called <u>to double-check</u> our flight. _____

4. She <u>leaps</u> out of bed in the morning. _____

5. I can play simple <u>tunes</u> on the piano. _____

B. Match each word to its meaning. Then write the letter next to the meaning on the line.

1. breathe _____   **a.** to ask for with force

2. attention _____   **b.** unwilling to wait

3. impatient _____   **c.** the act of watching or listening carefully

4. accident _____   **d.** to take air into your body

5. demand _____   **e.** a sad event that is not expected

Name _____

A. Write the word from the box to complete each sentence.

> gasped   leave   effort   emergency   flashlight   ancient

1. The police get _____ calls about accidents.

2. We were so startled we _____ in surprise.

3. This _____ art is more than two thousand years old.

4. During a fire drill, we must _____ the building.

5. The power failed, and I needed my _____!

6. Lea made a great _____ to study for the test.

B. Use the words in the box to complete the crossword puzzle.

> students   shark   buddy   unable

Across

1. friend

3. an ocean fish with a large mouth and sharp teeth

4. people who study

Down

2. not able

The vowel sound you hear in these words is followed by the **r** sound. The vowel sound is changed by the **r** that follows it.

You can hear the **ar** sound in **car** and **art**.

You can hear the **or** sound in **store** and **horn**.

Write a word from the box to complete each sentence.

farm	corn	sport	storm	dark

1. Basketball is my favorite _____.

2. We shut off all the lights so the room was completely

   _____.

3. The farmer harvested _____ and carrots.

4. The weatherman predicted there was going to be a

   _____ with lots of rain and lightning.

5. Laura visits her grandfather's _____ to see the cows, horses, and pigs.

© Macmillan/McGraw-Hill

At Home: Have your child brainstorm three more r-controlled words and use each one in a sentence.

Name _____

Choose words from the box to finish the animal reports. Write the words on the lines.

| itches | puddles | handy | preen | beasts | nibble |

Bears

Bears are _____ because they have four feet. They

are gentle and _____ on berries. Bears rub their

backs against trees to scratch their _____.

Birds

Birds have beaks that are _____ for picking

up food. They also use their beaks to _____ or

smooth their feathers. Birds take baths in _____.

Name _____

As you read *Splish! Splash! Animal Baths,* fill in the
Compare and Contrast Chart.

Animal:	Animal:	Animal:
Behavior	**Behavior**	**Behavior**

How does the information you wrote in this Compare and Contrast
Chart help you to better understand *Splish! Splash! Animal Baths*?

 At Home: Have your child use the chart to retell the story.

Splish! Splash! Animal Baths
Book 2.2/Unit 4 129

© Macmillan/McGraw-Hill

Name _____

When you **compare**, you tell how things are alike.

When you **contrast**, you tell how things are different.

A. Put a check in each box if it tells something about bears or about pigs. Then use the chart to talk about how bears and pigs are alike and different.

	bear	pig
lives on a farm		
is a mammal		
has a snout		
has fur		
has two small eyes		

B. Write a sentence comparing a bear and a pig. Then write a sentence contrasting a bear and a pig.

_____

_____

 At Home: Have your child tell you how dogs and cats are alike and how they are different.

© Macmillan/McGraw-Hill

Name _____

As I read, I will pay attention to the punctuation in each sentence.

	Giraffes are the tallest animals on Earth. They are
9	mammals. This means they have warm blood and hair
18	on their bodies. They feed their babies milk.
26	Giraffes look a bit like jigsaw puzzles. They are
35	tan–colored with brown patches. They have long legs, long
44	necks, and tiny horns. Giraffes live for 20 to 30 years.
53	Most giraffes live on the African savanna. This is a dry
64	grassland with few trees.
68	Giraffes share their home with many other animals.
76	Lions also live on the savanna. Sometimes they
84	hunt giraffes.
86	Tick birds live on the savanna. They are handy because
96	they eat insects that live in the giraffes' fur. This helps the
108	giraffes have fewer **itches** caused by insects. 115

Comprehension Check

1. What do lions and giraffes have in common? **Compare and Contrast**

2. How do you know giraffes are the tallest animals on the African savanna? **Make and Confirm Predictions**

	Words Read	–	Number of Errors	=	Words Correct Score
First Read		–		=	
Second Read		–		=	

At Home: Help your child read the passage, paying attention to the goal at the top of the page.

Splish! Splash! Animal Baths
Book 2.2/Unit 4

131

You can tell whether a noun is singular or plural by looking at its ending. Nouns that end with **–s** or **–es** are plural.

Read the story. Find the plural nouns. Write them on the lines. Then circle the ending in each noun you wrote.

We saw many animals on Mr. Brown's farm. There were horses in the field and pigs rolling in the mud. The ducks were near the lake and the hens were in the barn. I liked the baby chicks. Mrs. Brown made lunches for us to eat. We sat on the benches and ate them.

1. _____   2. _____

3. _____   4. _____

5. _____   6. _____

7. _____   8. _____

 At Home: Help your child read a storybook. Then ask him or her to point out any inflected nouns.

Name _____

Words are divided into **syllables.** A syllable is a word part. Each syllable has one vowel sound.

A. Circle the number that matches the number of syllables in each word.

1. smart

   1   2   3

2. corner

   1   2   3

3. anymore

   1   2   3

4. morning

   1   2   3

5. chore

   1   2   3

6. alarming

   1   2   3

7. fork

   1   2   3

8. charming

   1   2   3

9. barn

   1   2   3

10. harmony

    1   2   3

11. normal

    1   2   3

12. partner

    1   2   3

B. Write two sentences using *r*- controlled vowels.

13. _____

    _____

    _____

14. _____

    _____

© Macmillan/McGraw-Hill

 At Home: Name several words and have your child tell how many syllables are in each word.

> **Characters** are people or animals in a story or play.
>
> The **setting** is where and when a story or play happens.

Read the play. Then answer the questions.

Happy Birthday, Duck!

(in the forest, on a sunny morning)

Bear: Hi, Rabbit, what are you doing?

Rabbit: *(holding a cake)* Hi, Bear. I am waiting for Bird. We are going to visit Duck. Today is Duck's birthday. Would you like to come with us?

Bear: Sure. *(Bird walks into the forest.)*

Bear and Rabbit: Hi, Bird. Let's go to the lake to surprise Duck. *(The three walk to the lake.)*

Bear, Rabbit, and Bird: Good Morning, Duck. Happy Birthday!

Duck: Thank you! What a wonderful surprise!

1. How many characters are in the play? _____

2. Where is the play set? _____

3. When does the play happen? _____

4. What is Rabbit holding? _____

At Home: Ask your child to write a short play. Then have him or her create characters and a setting.

Name _____

The letters **er, ir,** and **ur** can sometimes stand for the same vowel sound.

Listen for the vowel sound as you say these words.

h**er**   f**ir**st   f**ur**

A. Read the words in the box below. Then circle the letters in each word that stand for the vowel sound.

turn   herd   curl   bird   term   girl

B. Write the words from the box that have the same vowel sound and spelling as the name of the picture.

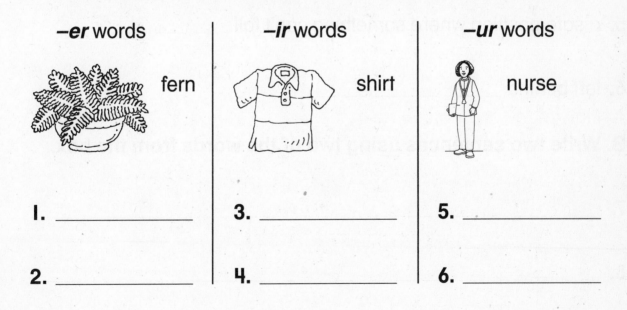

–*er* words   fern   –*ir* words   shirt   –*ur* words   nurse

1. _____   3. _____   5. _____

2. _____   4. _____   6. _____

© Macmillan/McGraw-Hill

At Home: Ask your child to write a sentence using the words
her, bird, and *turn.*

Name _____

A. Choose the correct word from the box to match each definition. Write the word on the line.

| wider   saddest   freezes   imagine   deserted   balance |

I. becomes solid because of cold _____

2. to picture something in the mind _____

3. the most unhappy _____

4. covering a larger area from side to side _____

5. a safe position where something can't fall _____

6. left behind _____

B. Write two sentences using two of the words from the box.

7. _____

8. _____

Name _____

As you read *Goose's Story*, fill in the Cause and
Effect Chart.

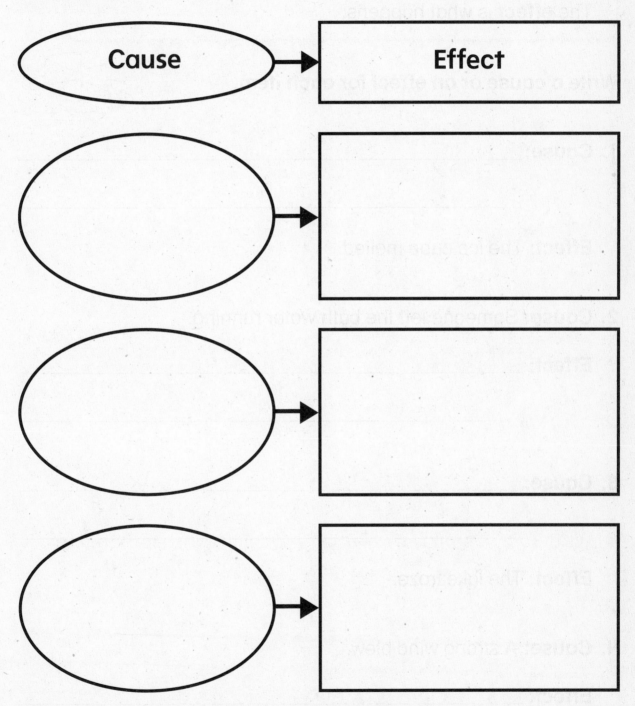

How does the information you wrote in this Cause and Effect Chart
help you to better understand *Goose's Story*?

At Home: Have your child use the chart to retell the story.

Goose's Story • Book 2.2/Unit 4   137

© Macmillan/McGraw-Hill

A **cause** is what makes something happen.

The **effect** is what happens.

Write a cause or an effect for each item.

1. **Cause:** _____

_____

   Effect: The ice cube melted.

2. **Cause:** Someone left the bath water running.

   Effect: _____

_____

3. **Cause:** _____

_____

   Effect: The lake froze.

4. **Cause:** A strong wind blew.

   Effect: _____

_____

© Macmillan/McGraw-Hill

At Home: With your child, say the *Little Miss Muffet* rhyme.
Then ask what caused Little Miss Muffet to feel frightened
and run away.

Name _____

As I read, I will pay attention to the punctuation in each sentence.

	Kenny and Grandfather sat together on the porch.
8	They could hear the frogs singing in the pond behind the fence.
20	"Have the frogs sung every summer?" Kenny asked Grandfather.
29	"Every summer," Grandfather told him. "Every year."
36	Kenny loved the pond. It was part of a wetland area where
48	waterbirds lived. Dragonflies buzzed in the grass and wild
57	ducks swam.
59	But tonight Grandfather had bad news.
65	"Big changes are coming," Grandfather told Kenny.
72	"What kind of changes?"
76	"As more people come to live here, they'll need more houses
87	and more roads."
90	Kenny was surprised. "Where will they build them?"
98	he asked. 100

Comprehension Check

1. Why will more houses and roads be built? **Cause and Effect**

2. What did Kenny love about the pond? **Make Inferences**

	Words Read	–	Number of Errors	=	Words Correct Score
First Read		–		=	
Second Read		–		=	

© Macmillan/McGraw-Hill

At Home: Help your child read the passage, paying attention to the goal at the top of the page.

You can use adjectives to compare.

Adjectives with **–er** compare **two** people, places, or things.

Adjectives with **–est** compare **more than two** people, places, or things.

Add –er or –est to the adjective in ( ). Write the new word on the line to complete each sentence.

1. The little hen works (hard) _____ than the big hen to keep its eggs safe.

2. The little hen has the (small) _____ nest of all the nests on the farm.

3. Ron's pig spends a (long) _____ time in the mud than Ann's pig does.

4. The horse runs (fast) _____ than the cow.

5. The rooster is the (loud) _____ of all the farm animals.

6. The blue bird can see worms from a (high) _____ spot than the hen can see them.

At Home: Ask your child to compare buildings or trees outside by telling you which are tall, taller, and tallest.

© Macmillan/McGraw-Hill

Name _____

When the letter **r** comes after a vowel, the vowel sounds different from the usual short or long sound.

Listen to the different vowel sounds in each word pair.

b**u**n   b**ur**n   f**i**st   f**ir**st   g**e**m   g**er**m

Circle the missing letters. Then write them to complete the word. Read the word.

1. er   ir

c ___ ___ cle

2. er   ir

k ___ ___ nel

3. ur   er

t ___ ___ tle

4. ur   er

p ___ ___ ch

5. ir   er

sk ___ ___ t

6. er   ur

h ___ ___ t

At Home: Ask your child to tell you a riddle whose answer is *bird*.

Name _____

A **map** is a drawing that shows where different places are. The **compass rose** on the map shows you directions north, south, east, and west.

Tracie and her family just moved to a new town. Use the map below to help them get around. Circle the best answer to each question.

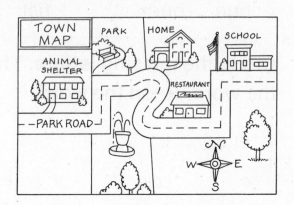

1. If Tracie wants to go to the park after school, which direction should she travel to get there?

    a. north   **b.** east   **c.** west

2. If Tracie wants to go home from the park, which direction should she travel to get there?

    a. south   **b.** west   **c.** east

3. Tracie and her family want to go out for dinner. How can they get to the restaurant from home?

    a. travel southeast   **b.** travel northeast   **c.** travel northwest

4. Tracie and her family want to volunteer at the animal shelter on weekends. How can they get to the animal shelter from home?

    a. go east and past the school   **b.** go west and through the park

At Home: Help your child draw a map of your street.

Name _____

The letters **oo** and **ou** can stand for the vowel sound you hear in **cook** and **should**.

A. Read each word. Write a new word that rhymes. Then underline the letters in each word that make the sound you hear in the middle of *cook* and *would*.

1. stood _____

2. shook _____

3. soot _____

4. could _____

5. brook _____

6. good _____

B. Write two sentences using two of the words you wrote above.

7. _____

8. _____

At Home: Have your child make up rhymes using the rhyming words in the left and right columns above.

A Way to Help Planet Earth
Book 2.2/Unit 4

143

Name _____

Use a word from the box to complete each clue. Then write your answers in the puzzle.

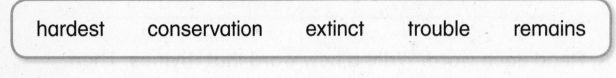

hardest   conservation   extinct   trouble   remains

Across

2. _____ are what is left of an animal's body after it has died.

3. An animal that is _____ has died out forever.

5. You would have less _____ if you followed directions.

Down

1. Using as little water as you can is good _____.

4. Diamonds are the _____ kind of stone.

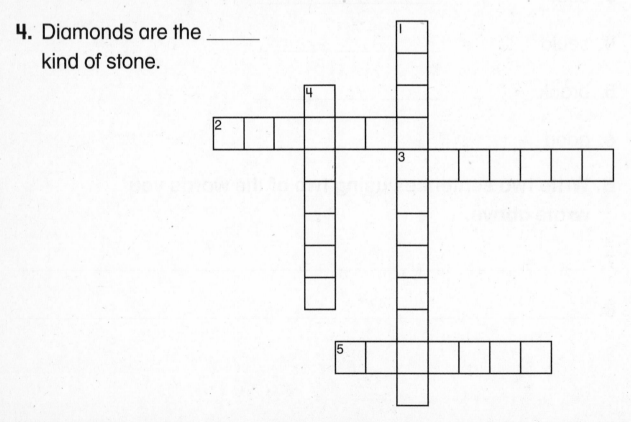

As you read *A Way to Help Planet Earth*, fill in the Description Web.

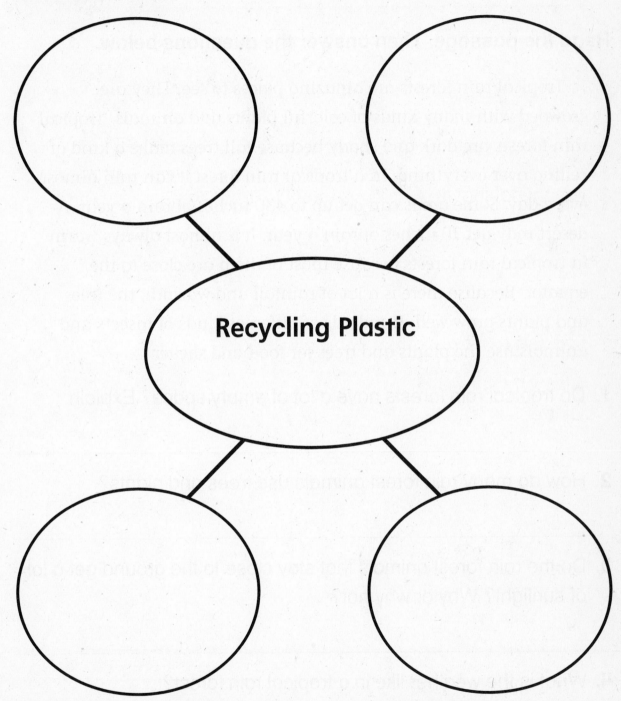

Recycling Plastic

How does the information you wrote in this Description Web help you to better understand *A Way to Help Planet Earth*?

 At Home: Have your child use the chart to retell the story.

A Way to Help Planet Earth
Book 2.2/Unit 4   145

© Macmillan/McGraw-Hill

Name _____

A **description** tells what a person, place, or thing is like.

Read the passage. Then answer the questions below.

Tropical rain forests are amazing places to see. They are crowded with many kinds of colorful plants and animals. Tropical rain forests are dark and shady because tall trees make a kind of ceiling over everything. In a tropical rain forest it can rain almost every day. Some areas can get up to 430 inches of rain a year. A desert may get 10 inches of rain a year. It is almost always warm in tropical rain forests because most of them are close to the equator. Because there is a lot of rainfall and warmth, the trees and plants grow well. Hundreds of different kinds of insects and animals use the plants and trees for food and shelter.

1. Do tropical rain forests have a lot of empty space? Explain.

_____

2. How do many rain forest animals use trees and plants?

_____

3. Do the rain forest animals that stay close to the ground get a lot of sunlight? Why or why not?

_____

4. What is the weather like in a tropical rain forest?

_____

At Home: Give a short oral description of a place you have seen but your child has not. Then have him or her ask questions about the place you have described.

You can use context clues to help figure out what and how things are being compared.

Read the passage. Then answer the questions below.

West Lakes Wildlife Park is a protected place where animals live. Many bison live here. No other animal here is as tall and heavy as the bison. Some big elks live here, too. There are also some deer living here. An adult deer comes up to an elk's shoulder. One of our deer weighs only about half as much as an elk. Other animals live here, too. Some are large, and some are small. Come on in and see them all!

1. What is the **biggest** animal at this wildlife park? _____

2. Underline the context clue or clues that helped you to figure out the answer to question 1.

3. Which is **bigger,** an elk or a deer? _____

4. Circle the context clues that helped you to figure out the answer to question 3.

5. Can you tell from the passage what the **smallest** animal at the park is? Explain your answer. _____

_____

_____

_____

 At Home: Put three common household items of different sizes in a row. Then have your child practice comparing the sizes using adjectives that end in *-er* or *-est*.

Name _____

You can use **text features** and **changes in print** to get information. A **caption** is a short label that tells about a picture. A **sidebar** can be a shorter story, a chart or graph, or a picture that is placed next to the main article. **Bold type** is heavy, dark type. *Italic type* slants to the right. Authors use these features to call attention to important words.

Read the article below. Then answer the questions.

How Can We Care for the Land?
Planting trees can help care for the land.
Recycling paper, glass, cans, and plastic can help care for the land.
More ways to help care for the land can be found in the book *What I Can Do to Help*.

planting trees

recycling

1. Underline the title of this article.

2. How is the title different from the rest of the text? _____

_____

3. Draw a box around the words below the title that the author wants to call special attention to.

4. What kind of information is in the sidebar? _____

_____

At Home: Together, look through magazines and newspapers and identify examples of the text features listed above.

Name _____

As I read, I will pay attention to the pronunciation of vocabulary words.

	Sometimes there is an oil spill. This may happen
9	because the tanker has an accident. Or the tanker may
19	be caught in a natural disaster, such as a hurricane.
29	In an oil spill, most of the oil floats on the water.
41	It spreads very quickly. It forms a layer called an oil
52	slick. The more the oil spreads, the thinner the layer
62	becomes.
63	Then winds and ocean waves carry the oil toward
72	the shore. The oil covers the rocks and sand on the
83	beach.
84	Even a small spill means big **trouble**. It can kill
94	hundreds of animals. A large spill can kill thousands!
103	When oil spills happen, endangered animals are at
111	risk of becoming **extinct**. 115

Comprehension Check

1. What happens when a tanker has an oil spill? **Description**

2. How can a large oil spill cause animals to become extinct?
   Cause and Effect

	Words Read	–	Number of Errors	=	Words Correct Score
First Read		–		=	
Second Read		–		=	

At Home: Help your child read the passage, paying attention to the goal at the top of the page.

Rules for Breaking Words into Syllables	
Words with two consonants between two vowels usually break between the consonants.	af-ter
Words with a consonant between a short vowel and another vowel usually break after the consonant.	riv-er
Words with a consonant between a long vowel and another vowel usually break before the consonant.	ho-tel
Compound words break between the two shorter words.	drive-way
Words with suffixes or prefixes break between the root word and the suffix or prefix.	use-less, re-read
Words with word endings *-s*, *-'s*, or *-ed* usually have no break except *-ed* after *d* or *t*.	Jen's, rained, want-ed

Rewrite each word. Put hyphens (-) between the syllables. If the word has only one syllable, rewrite the word with no hyphens.

1. somewhere _____ 2. reran _____

3. bookbag _____ 4. button _____

5. hinted _____ 6. hooked _____

7. heavy _____ 8. could _____

At Home: Write words that fit the patterns described above. Then help your child identify which pattern applies, and work together to break the words into syllables.

© Macmillan/McGraw-Hill

The letters *oo, ui, ew, ue,* and *oe* can make the same vowel sound.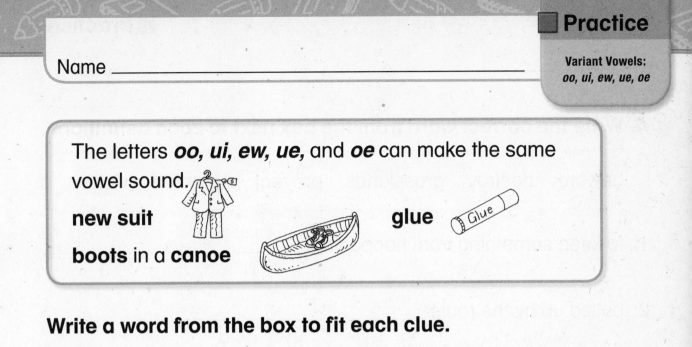

new suit

boots in a **canoe**

glue

Write a word from the box to fit each clue.

kangaroo	blue	shoes	hoot	fruit
juice	glue	canoe	flew	chew

1. This is the sound an owl makes. _____

2. This is something to wear on your feet. _____

3. A bird did this to get to the top of a tree. _____

4. Apples and grapes belong to this food group. _____

5. The sky can be this color. _____

6. This animal hops, but it is not a rabbit. _____

7. This is a kind of boat. _____

8. This is something you can drink. _____

 At Home: Help your child make up sentences for the words in the box that were not used on the page.

Super Storms • Book 2.2/Unit 4   151

A. Write the correct word from the box next to each definition.

beware   destroy   grasslands   prevent   uprooted   violent

1. to keep something from happening: ___ ___ ___ ___ ___ ___ ___
                                            II   4

2. pulled up by the roots: ___ ___ ___ ___ ___ ___ ___ ___
                              3   10   9

3. to ruin completely: ___ ___ ___ ___ ___ ___ ___
                          5   8

4. lands covered with grass, where animals feed:

   ___ ___ ___ ___ ___ ___ ___ ___ ___ ___
        7

5. happening with or because of a strong force

   ___ ___ ___ ___ ___ ___ ___
                    I

6. to be on one's guard: ___ ___ ___ ___ ___ ___
                                              6

B. Write the numbered letters from your answers on the lines below to find the answer to the riddle.

Beware of me! I can be **violent**, **destroy** buildings, **uproot** trees, and damage **grasslands.** What am I?

___ H ___ ___ ___ ___ ___ ___ ___ ___ M ___
 I 2 3 4 5 6 7 8 9 10 II 12

As you read *Super Storms*, fill in the Predictions Chart.

What I Predict	What Happens

How does the information you wrote in this Predictions Chart help you to better understand *Super Storms*?

© Macmillan/McGraw-Hill

At Home: Have your child use the chart to retell the story.

Super Storms • Book 2.2/Unit 4 153

When you **make a prediction**, you use information from the story and what you already know to make a good guess about what will happen next.

Read each story. Then answer the question.

Jorge didn't like going out in the rain, but it was his turn to walk the dog. Jorge put on his raincoat, rain boots, and rain hat, and picked up the leash.

1. What do you think Jorge will do next? _____

_____

Leslie stirred the soup in a pot on the stove. Allison made a salad. Louie set the table and looked at the clock again. Just then, Mom walked in. "Hi, kids," she called, "sorry, I'm late."

2. What do you think the family will do next? _____

_____

It is a cloudy afternoon, but not raining. Ms. Sherman takes her class to the playground. Eva and Nathan play catch. Mark hangs from the monkey bars. Ms. Sherman keeps an eye on the sky. Suddenly they hear the rumble of thunder.

3. What do you think the class will do next? _____

_____

At Home: Ask your child to predict the next thing that will happen in each story.

Name _____

As I read, I will pay attention to the pronunciation of the vocabulary words and tempo.

12	Suddenly Abby felt the air get cooler. She stood up and looked at the sea. Abby saw big, black clouds moving in the sky.
24	"Better **beware**! A great big storm is coming this way!"
34	Abby cried out.
37	Then the wind blew in. A **violent** gust took them all by
49	surprise! They couldn't **prevent** their towels from flying up in
59	the air. Wild weather was on its way. Fudge ran around in circles.
72	As the family packed up the picnic, sand blew in their faces.
84	Waves were quickly rolling onto the beach.
91	Lightning flashed over the sea. Thunder rumbled, closer and
100	closer.
101	"Look!" shouted Jack. "The tree is being **uprooted** by the
111	storm!" 112

Comprehension Check

1. How did Abby know a big storm was coming? **Make and Confirm Predictions**

2. What caused the towels to fly up in the air? **Cause and Effect**

	Words Read	–	Number of Errors	=	Words Correct Score
First Read		–		=	
Second Read		–		=	

© Macmillan/McGraw-Hill

 At Home: Help your child read the passage, paying attention to the goal at the top of the page.

A **compound word** is a word that is made up of two smaller words. You can often figure out the meaning of a compound word by thinking about the meanings of the smaller words.

rain + coat = raincoat   snow + suit = snowsuit

Read each sentence. Circle the compound word. Then write its meaning on the line.

1. Big, fluffy snowflakes fell during the blizzard yesterday.

_____

2. The strong wind made the sailboats speed across the water.

_____

3. The storm made the power go out, so we ate dinner by candlelight.

_____

4. The heavy rain and loud thunder make thunderstorms scary.

_____

5. Be sure to wipe your muddy shoes on the doormat.

_____

At Home: Have your child look around the house for things with names that are compound words, such as bedspread. Then help him or her use the words in sentences.

Name _____

> The letters **oo, ui, oe, ue,** and **ew** can make the same vowel sound. Sometimes the same sound can be spelled in different ways. Listen to the vowel sounds as you say these words: b**oo**t   s**ui**t   sh**oe**   bl**ue**   n**ew**

Circle the word that has the same vowel sound as the name of the picture.

1. glue   foot   would   kangaroo

2. took   smooth   town   fruit

3. blew   shook   push   tooth

4. cut   juice   full   moose

5. canoe   fur   could   spacesuit

6. good   took   zoom   balloon

At Home: Have your child write a sentence for the words that he or she circled.

© Macmillan/McGraw-Hill

> **Repetition** is when one word or phrase appears two or more times in a poem.
>
> **Word choice** is important in a poem. The words a poet chooses gives the poem a certain feeling or mood.

Read the nursery rhyme. Then answer the questions below.

Three little kittens lost their mittens,
And they began to cry,
Oh, mother dear, we sadly fear,
Our mittens we have lost.

Lost your mittens! You naughty kittens!
Then you shall have no pie.
Meow, meow! Meow, meow!
Then you shall have no pie.

1. What words are repeated in this rhyme? _____

_____

2. What is the mood in the first verse? _____

3. Which words or lines help create the mood of the first verse?

_____

4. What is the mood in the second verse? _____

5. Which words or lines help create the mood of the second verse?

_____

© Macmillan/McGraw-Hill

At Home: Read other poems and rhymes with your child
and have him or her identify the words that create the mood.

The letters *au* and *aw* often have the same sound. You can hear the sound of *au* in *caught* and *aw* in *claw*.

Choose the word from the box that best matches each picture and clue. Then write it on the line below.

| sauce | yawn | laundry | straw | sausage |

 I. This is clothing that needs to be washed.

_____

 2. This is something that can help you drink.

_____

 **3.** This can be good with spaghetti. _____

 **4.** You may do this when you are tired.

_____

 **5.** You might eat this for breakfast. _____

 At Home: Write words with *au* and *aw* on index cards. Then shuffle the cards and have your child sort them by vowel pair.

Name _____

Choose the word from the box to complete each sentence. Then write the word on the line.

| glanced | beloved | promised | noble | gleamed | wiggled |

1. Aunt Linda lives in a farmhouse with her _____ pigs, Princess and Queeny.

2. I _____ to visit when school lets out for the summer.

3. I _____ at the pictures of my last visit to her farm.

4. Queeny wore a diamond collar that _____ in the light.

5. Princess _____ around in mud to keep cool.

6. Although pigs like to roll around in the mud, I think they are very

_____ animals.

As you read *Nutik, the Wolf Pup*, fill in the Inference Chart.

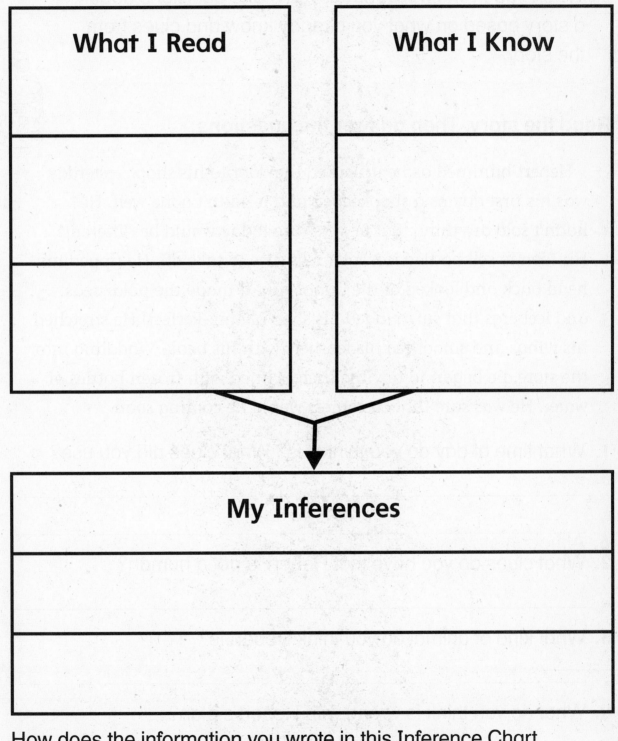

What I Read	What I Know

My Inferences

How does the information you wrote in this Inference Chart
help you to better understand *Nutik, the Wolf Pup*?

© Macmillan/McGraw-Hill

At Home: Have your child use the chart to retell the story.

Nutik, the Wolf Pup • **Book 2.2/Unit 4**   161

When you **make inferences**, you make decisions about a story based on what you already know and clues from the story.

Read the story. Then answer the questions.

Hebert hummed as he unlocked the door to his shop. Yesterday was his first day as a shopkeeper, and it hadn't gone well. He hadn't sold anything. But he was sure today would be different! His idea to sell bottled ice water was sure to take off. He tipped his head back and looked at the bright sun. It made the polar seas and icebergs that surrounded his shop gleam. Perfect! He stretched his wings and smoothed his feathers with his beak. Waddling into the store, he began to tidy the shelves lined with frozen bottles of water. He was sure that customers would be coming soon.

1. What time of day do you think it is? What clues did you use?

_____

_____

2. What clues do you have that Hebert is not a human?

_____

3. What kind of animal do you think Hebert is?

_____

4. What do you think is wrong with Hebert's plan?

_____

 At Home: As you read together, have your child share with you what he or she has "guessed" about the story so far.

Name _____

As I read, I will pay attention and copy tone and expression.

	A coral reef is like a big city under the water. Thousands
12	of sea creatures live around a coral reef.
20	Coral reefs grow in shallow, warm seas. They grow all
30	over the world.
33	Tiny animals called polyps (*PAHL-ips*) build corals. Each
40	polyp makes a hard coral cup to use as a home. Millions of
53	cups form a coral reef.
58	Corals come in all shapes and sizes. Staghorn coral looks
68	like spiky purple antlers. Plate coral looks like a large dinner
79	plate. Brain coral looks like a big brain.
87	Fish love coral reefs because there is plenty of food.
97	Parrotfish crunch on the coral with their sharp teeth.
106	Lionfish have red and white stripes. They also have long
116	fins and spines. Lionfish use their long spines to trap small
127	fish against the coral. 131

Comprehension Check

1. Why do fish love coral reefs? **Make Inferences**

2. How are coral reefs like big underwater cities? **Make and Confirm Predictions**

	Words Read	–	Number of Errors	=	Words Correct Score
First Read		–		=	
Second Read		–		=	

© Macmillan/McGraw-Hill

At Home: Help your child read the passage, paying attention to the goal at the top of the page.

Name _____

A **verb** is an action word. To show that action takes
place in the past, **-ed** is added to the verb.

**Underline the verb in each sentence. Then change each
verb so that it tells about the past. Write the new word on
the line.**

1. I wash the dog on Saturdays. _____

2. My parents clean the yard. _____

3. I love my science class. _____

4. The teachers plan our class parties. _____

5. We like the new teacher. _____

6. Puppies wag their tails. _____

7. The students talk about the class trip. _____

8. We hope for sunny skies. _____

At Home: Look for verbs that end in *-ing* or *-ed* in the stories
you read together. Then help your child find the base word in
the inflected verb.

Name _____

The letter pairs *au* and *aw* often make the same sound. You can hear the sound of *au* and *aw* in *August* and *paw*.

A. Use a word from the box to complete each sentence.

sauce	autumn	yawn	fault	hawk	draw

1. The leaves fall in the _____.

2. The _____ flew high overhead.

3. I like to eat noodles with _____.

4. It was an accident so it was not my _____.

5. I _____ when I am tired.

B. There is one word in the box that you have not used. Use it in a sentence. Write it on the lines.

6. _____

_____

 At Home: Have your child find words with *au* and *aw* in books and magazines.

Nutik, the Wolf Pup • Book 2.2/Unit 4   165

Name _____

Suppose you have a research assignment. You have to write a one-page paper on one animal. Think about this assignment as you answer each question below.

1. Circle the topic that best fits the assignment.

arctic animals   polar bears   fish

2. Which reference material would be the best one to use?

encyclopedia   dictionary   atlas

3. Why is your choice the best reference material for the assignment?

_____

_____

_____

The encyclopedia article on your animal has sections with the following heads:

Appearance   Habitat   Diet

4. In which section would you find information about what your

animal eats? _____

5. Which section may include a photo of your animal?

_____

6. Which section may include a map that shows where your animal

lives? _____

At Home: Look at different encyclopedia entries with your child and talk about the kinds of information the heads provide.

Name _____

A. Write a word from the box to complete each caption.

| freezes | extinct | itches | preen |

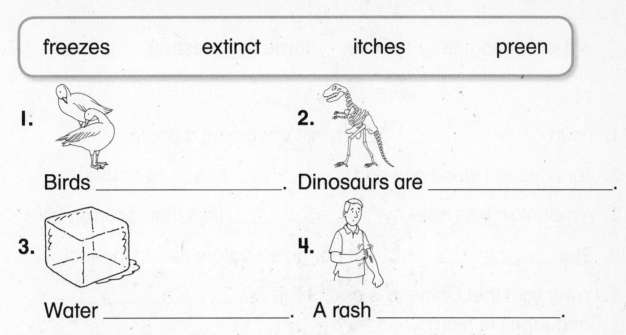

1.

Birds _____.

2.

Dinosaurs are _____.

3.

Water _____.

4.

A rash _____.

B. Match each clue to the correct word. Then write the letter next to the word on the line.

1. wild animals _____   **a.** uprooted

2. to keep from happening _____   **b.** juice

3. pulled out of the ground _____   **c.** gleamed

4. made a vow _____   **d.** prevent

5. squeeze oranges for this _____   **e.** beasts

6. sparkled in the light _____   **f.** promised

A. Write a word from the box to complete each sentence.

| wider | imagine | trouble | hardest | destroy | glanced |

1. I can _____ myself becoming a doctor.

2. Termites eat wood and can _____ a house.

3. A mountain bike has _____ tires than a racing bike.

4. She _____ at her notes before taking the test.

5. Yung said that Chinese is one of the _____
   languages to learn.

6. Carl's sister had _____ writing with a cast
   on her broken arm.

B. Circle and then write the word that completes each sentence.

1. I was _____ in July.

   torn   horn   born

2. I love to _____ pictures of animals.

   draw   taught   hawk

3. My cat sheds a lot of _____.

   fern   fur   bird

4. It is my turn to help _____ dinner.

   foot   cook   could

Two letter sounds blended together can make one vowel sound. Sometimes the letters **ow** or **ou** can stand for the same vowel sound. You can hear the sound of **ou** in **house** and the sound of **ow** in **cow**.

Read each word. Then circle the word next to it that has the same vowel sound.

1. south   toy
              clown

2. ground   wow
               tool

3. sound   now
              one

4. shower   show
               pound

5. power   out
              point

6. clown   round
              soil

7. cloud   grow
              brown

8. loud   loyal
             town

9. how   mow
            ouch

10. howl   mouth
               own

At Home: Ask your child to say words that rhyme with the words that he or she circled.

© Macmillan/McGraw-Hill

Name _____

Choose a word from the box to finish each sentence.
Then write the word on the line.

| ranger's   lengthy   beyond   burrow   warning   distant |

1. Mark ran so quickly that he ran _____ the finish line.

2. Scientists study _____ stars and planets.

3. Many desert animals can spend _____ periods of time without water.

4. There was a _____ to all hikers to stay inside because of the sand storm.

5. A desert tortoise can dig an underground _____ to escape the heat.

6. The hiking trail started at the _____ station and ended at the top of the mountain.

© Macmillan/McGraw-Hill

Name _____

As you read *Dig, Wait, Listen: A Desert Toad's Tale,* fill in the Author's Purpose Chart.

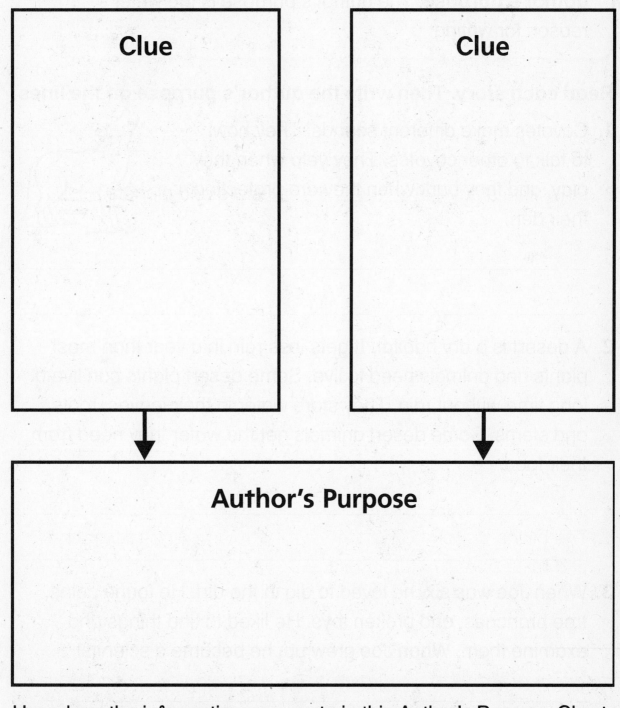

Clue	Clue

Author's Purpose

How does the information you wrote in this Author's Purpose Chart help you summarize *Dig, Wait, Listen: A Desert Toad's Tale*?

 At Home: Have your child use the chart to retell the story.

One way to summarize a selection is to think about the **author's purpose**. The author's purpose is the writer's reason for writing.

Read each story. Then write the author's purpose on the lines.

1. Coyotes make different sounds. They howl to talk to other coyotes. They yelp when they play, and they bark when they are protecting their den.

_____

_____

2. A desert is a dry habitat. It gets less rain in a year than most plants and animals need to live. Some desert plants can live a long time without rain. They store water in their leaves, roots, and stems. Some desert animals get the water they need from their food.

_____

_____

3. When Joe was six, he loved to dig in the dirt. He found coins, tree branches, and broken toys. He liked to find things and examine them. When Joe grew up, he became a scientist.

_____

_____

At Home: Have your child read a storybook and summarize it. Then ask your child to tell you the author's purpose.

© Macmillan/McGraw-Hill

As I read, I will pay attention to tone and expression.

	Australia is the driest continent in the world. It has
10	10 deserts.
11	All deserts are very dry. They are hot during the day, and
23	cold at night. But many plants and animals have adapted to
34	life in the desert.
38	People live in the Australian desert, too. The Aboriginal
47	[ab-uh-RIJ-i-nuhl] people have lived in the Australian
53	desert for 40,000 years.
56	The red kangaroo lives in the Australian desert. A female
66	can carry its young in a pouch, or pocket, on its stomach.
78	Kangaroos are marsupials. There are more than 200
85	kinds of marsupials that live in or near Australia.
94	Most desert marsupials, such as the numbat, are small. They
104	can dig into the sand and hide under rocks or in trees. 116

Comprehension Check

1. What does the author want you to know? **Author's Purpose**

2. How is Australia different from all other continents? **Compare and Contrast**

	Words Read	−	Number of Errors	=	Words Correct Score
First Read		−		=	
Second Read		−		=	

At Home: Help your child read the passage, paying attention to the goal at the top of the page.

Practice

Vocabulary Strategy:
Possessives

Name _____

A word that shows who or what owns something is a
possessive noun. Many possessive nouns are formed
by adding an apostrophe(') and **s**.

**Choose the possessive from the box that best completes
the sentence. Then write it on the line.**

giraffe's   teacher's   dad's   bird's   dentist's   rabbit's

1. I borrowed chalk from the _____ desk.

2. Two eggs were in the _____ nest.

3. I waited to get my teeth checked at the _____
office.

4. The fox tried to enter the _____ burrow.

5. I used my _____ tools to fix my toy car.

6. Can you believe how long

the _____ neck is?

© Macmillan/McGraw-Hill

At Home: Read a storybook with your child. Then have him or
her look for any possessives in the story and point them out.

> **Synonyms** are words that have the same or nearly the same meaning.
>
> **Antonyms** are words that have the opposite or nearly the opposite meaning.

Choose a synonym or an antonym from the box for each underlined word. Use it in a sentence. Then write an _A_ next to the sentence if you used an antonym or an _S_ next to the sentence if you used a synonym.

> couch   shout   loud   gown   sound

1. Lori's cat likes to lie on the <u>sofa</u>.

_____

2. When I am trying to be quiet, I <u>whisper</u>.

_____

3. Jenna wore a beautiful <u>dress</u> to the party.

_____

4. The washing machine made a swishing <u>noise.</u>

_____

5. Tapping on the drums makes a <u>quiet</u> noise.

_____

At Home: Ask your child to name a synonym and an
antonym for the following words: *new, long,* and *late.*
Then ask him or her to use each word in a sentence.

Dig, Wait, Listen
Book 2.2/Unit 5   175

A **chart** gives information in a clear way. Information is often organized under headings. It is often easier to read facts in a chart than in a paragraph.

Use the information from the chart to answer the questions.

Desert Spadefoot Toads		
Where They Are Found	**Characteristics**	**Other Facts**
Sonoran Desert	olive gray to brown color	eat insects
underground	pale belly	nocturnal
on land or in water	short limbs	lay eggs
	amphibian	

1. In which desert can you find the spadefoot toad? _____

2. What color are the spadefoot toads? _____

3. What do they eat? _____

4. How would you describe the limbs of the toads?

_____

© Macmillan/McGraw-Hill

Name _____

The letters **oi** and **oy** can stand for the vowel sound you hear in the words **joy** and **noise**.

Write the missing letters in each word. Then read the word.

1.

c __ __ n s

2.

b __ __

3.

p __ __ n t

4.

b __ __ l

5.

t __ __ s

6.

__ __ l

 At Home: Have your child write three sentences using the words from above.

Name _____

A. Choose the word from the box that best matches each meaning below. Write the word on the line.

| jabbing | agreed | randomly | signal | gathered |

1. understood or had the same idea _____

2. a sign or warning _____

3. fast, sharp pushing _____

4. brought together _____

5. with no clear pattern _____

B. Write three sentences with words from the box.

6. _____

_____

7. _____

_____

8. _____

_____

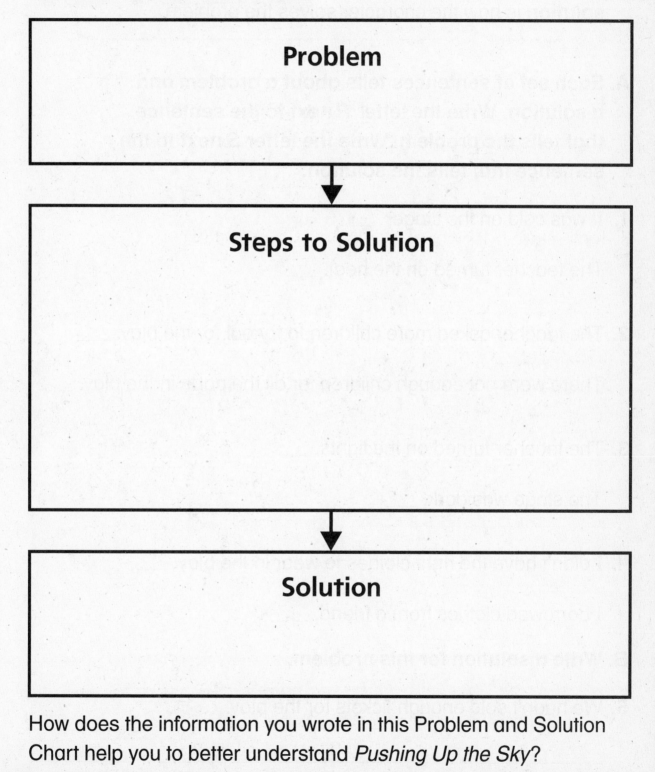
Name _____

As you read *Pushing Up the Sky,* **fill in the Problem and Solution Chart.**

Problem

↓

Steps to Solution

↓

Solution

How does the information you wrote in this Problem and Solution Chart help you to better understand *Pushing Up the Sky*?

At Home: Have your child use the chart to retell the story.

Name _____

In most stories, the main character has a **problem**. The **solution** is how the character solves the problem.

A. Each set of sentences tells about a problem and a solution. Write the letter *P* next to the sentence that tells the problem. Write the letter *S* next to the sentence that tells the solution.

1. It was cold on the stage. ____

The teacher turned on the heat. ____

2. The teacher asked more children to try out for the play. ____

There were not enough children for all the parts in the play. ____

3. The teacher turned on the lights. ____

The stage was dark. ____

4. I didn't have the right clothes to wear in the play. ____

I borrowed clothes from a friend. ____

B. Write a solution for this problem.

5. We hadn't sold enough tickets for the play.

_____

At Home: Ask your child how he or she would solve the problem of not knowing how to prepare a fruit salad.

Name _____

As I read, I will pay attention and copy tone and expression.

14	**Narrator:** This is a play based on a folk tale from Nigeria. A long time ago the Sky was very close to Earth. Whenever people were
26	hungry, they reached up **randomly** and broke off a piece of the Sky.
39	**Villager 1:** Mmm, tastes like corn.
44	**Villager 2:** Mmm, tastes like roasted potatoes.
50	**Villager 3:** Mmm, tastes like pineapple.
55	**Narrator:** The Sky tasted different to everyone. But all the
65	people agreed it was delicious.
70	**Narrator:** The people never had to work for food. They spent their
82	time making beautiful art, telling stories, and having festivals.
91	**Villager 1:** How many guests will King Oba invite to the
101	next festival?
103	**Villager 2:** 40!
104	**Villager 3:** 80!
105	**Child 1:** 100! 100!
106	**Narrator:** At festival time King Oba's servants made feasts from
116	pieces of the Sky. 120

Comprehension Check

1. What did the sky taste like? **Compare and Contrast**

2. According to the folk tale, how was the world different a long time ago? **Description**

	Words Read	–	Number of Errors	=	Words Correct Score
First Read		–		=	
Second Read		–		=	

At Home: Help your child read the passage, paying attention to the goal at the top of the page.

> You can add **endings** to a **base word** to make new words. The endings can change the meaning of the base word.

A. Read each word. Circle the base word. Draw a line under the ending. Then write the word in a sentence on the line.

1. helped

_____

2. fixing

_____

3. slowly

_____

B. Add the ending to the base word to make a new word. Write the word on the line. Then write the new word in a sentence.

4. go + ing = _____

_____

5. cook + ed = _____

_____

6. quiet + ly = _____

_____

At Home: Ask your child to add the endings *-ed* and *-ing* to
the base word *play*. Then have him or her write a sentence
that includes each new word.

© Macmillan/McGraw-Hill

Sometimes the letter **a** stands for the sound /ə/ (uh). This is called the **schwa** sound. You can hear the schwa sound at the beginning of the word **ago** and at the end of the word **papa**.   **a**go   pap**a**

Write the word from the box that answers each riddle.

alone	again	alike	agree
above	awake	pizza	mama

1. This means **one more time**. What word is it? _____

2. This is something good to eat. What word is it? _____

3. People do this when they think the same way about something.

What word is it? _____

4. This is another word for mother. What is it? _____

5. Two things are the same. What word is it? _____

6. This means **not asleep**. What word is it? _____

7. This means **all by yourself**. What word is it? _____

8. This is the opposite of **below**. What word is it? _____

At Home: Help your child make up a riddle for the word *ahead.*

Columbus Explores New Lands
Book 2.2/Unit 5

 185

Name _____

A. Draw a line to match each word with its definition.

1. oceans

2. planet

3. voyage

4. vast

5. areas

a. places, or sections of a place

b. very big; huge

c. a large object in space that travels around the Sun

d. huge bodies of salt water

e. a long trip by sea, air, or land

B. Write three sentences using all the words from the box above.

6. _____

_____

7. _____

_____

8. _____

_____

As you read *Columbus Explores New Lands*, fill
in the Main Idea and Details Web.

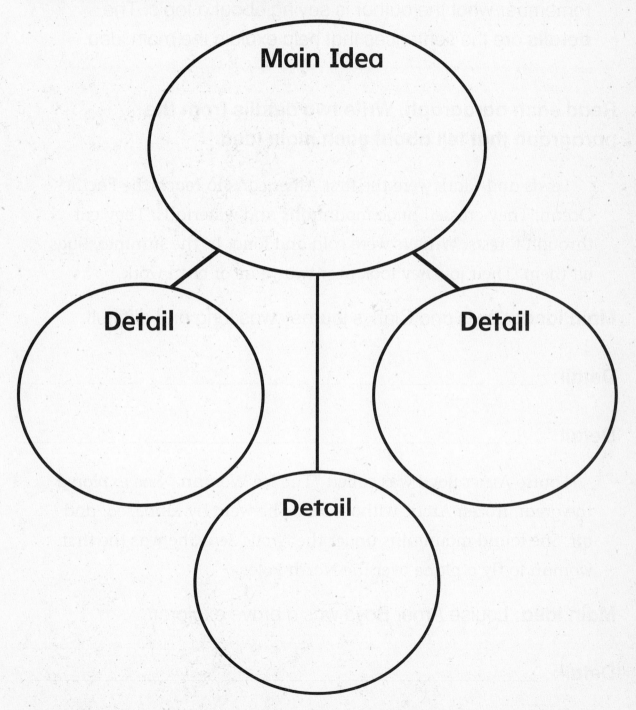

Main Idea

Detail

Detail

Detail

How does the information you wrote in this Main Idea and Details
Web help you summarize *Columbus Explores New Lands*?

 At Home: Have your child use the chart to retell the story.

Columbus Explores New Lands
Book 2.2/Unit 5

187

Learning how to identify the **main idea** will help you remember what the author is saying about a topic. The **details** are the sentences that help explain the main idea.

Read each paragraph. Write two details from the paragraph that tell about each main idea.

Lewis and Clark were the first Americans to reach the Pacific Ocean. They crossed huge mountains and waterfalls. They cut through forests. Winters were cold and long. In the summer, bugs bit them. Their journey took over two years of hard work.

Main idea: Lewis and Clark's journey was long and difficult.

Detail: _____

Detail: _____

Louise Arner Boyd was called "The Ice Woman." She explored the great, frozen Arctic without fear. She went by land, sea, and air. She found mountains under the Arctic Sea. She was the first woman to fly a plane over the North Pole.

Main idea: Louise Arner Boyd was a brave explorer.

Detail: _____

Detail: _____

© Macmillan/McGraw-Hill

 At Home: Have your child find one more detail in each paragraph that tells about the main idea.

If you see a group of unfamiliar words, think about what they might have in common. Also look at the other words in the paragraph for clues.

A. Read the paragraph. Then circle the best answers.

Imagine that you are a member of the Algonquin tribe. In the winter you wear <u>pibon-makizin</u> on your feet. They keep your feet warm. You also wear some <u>ajigans</u> inside your boots. You wear a <u>wiwikwan</u> on your head. In the summer you wear a <u>kabashimowayan</u> to go swimming.

I. What are pibon-makizin?

   a. warm mittens

   b. winter boots

2. What are ajigans?

   a. socks

   b. toys

3. What is a wiwikwan?

   a. hat

   b. warm mittens

4. What is a kabashimowayan?

   a. tee-shirt

   b. bathing suit

B. Write a sentence to answer both questions.

5. What do all the underlined words have in common?

_____

6. How is a kabashimowayan different from the other items?

_____

At Home: Have your child draw pictures that show the meaning of each underlined word in the paragraph.

You can use the **Internet** to do research. A **search engine** is a program on the Internet that helps you find information on the World Wide Web. A **URL** is the address of a Web site. A **home page** is the main page of a Web site.

Jess entered the key words *Columbus* and *voyage* on an Internet search engine. Use her search results to answer the questions below.

Search Engine **Kidlookup**

All About Christopher Columbus The life of **Columbus**, and his **voyage** of 1492 http://www.columbuslifeand voyage.com/	Visit Columbus, Ohio Hey, kids: Visit the city of **Columbus**, Ohio. This site will make your **voyage** a lot of fun! http://visitcolumbus.com/	New World Explorers Find out who explored America first. Read about the **voyage** of **Columbus**. Learn about Native American explorers, Cortez, Lewis and Clark, and others. http://newworldexplorers.com/

1. What is the name of the search engine that Jess used?

_____

2. What is the URL of the site **All About Christopher Columbus**?

_____

3. Which Web site would be best for learning whether other explorers came to America before Columbus?

_____

4. Which Web site would not help Jess to learn about Christopher Columbus? _____

Columbus? _____

© Macmillan/McGraw-Hill

At Home: Ask your child for some ideas about what to type into a search engine to learn more about what America was like before Columbus came.

As I read, I will pay attention to the pronunciation of the vocabulary words.

	If you travel south as far as you can go, you will reach
13	the South Pole. The South Pole is in Antarctica. Antarctica is
24	a continent covered with ice and snow. It is the coldest place
36	on Earth.
38	Strong winds blow across Antarctica. It does not rain.
47	It does not even snow very much.
54	A **vast** layer of ice, called an ice cap, covers the land. It is
68	more than a mile (about 2 kilometers) thick. The ice cap
78	extends into the sea.
82	The temperature in Antarctica is usually well below
90	32°F (0°C). Water freezes at this temperature. So ice and snow
101	don't melt in Antarctica.
105	Very few animals live in Antarctica. But many animals live
115	in the **oceans** around the ice cap for part of the year. 127

Comprehension Check

1. What is the weather like in Antarctica? **Main Idea and Details**

2. Why don't the ice and snow melt in Antarctica? **Description**

	Words Read	–	Number of Errors	=	Words Correct Score
First Read		–		=	
Second Read		–		=	

At Home: Help your child read the passage, paying attention to the goal at the top of the page.

Columbus Explores New Lands
Book 2.2/Unit 5

191

**A. Circle a word to complete each sentence.
Then write the word on the line.**

1. Sara and Anna both love to eat _____.

   a. about   **b.** comma   **c.** pizza

2. They both _____ apples, too.

   a. alarm   **b.** adore   **c.** ahead

3. The two girls ate lunch together _____ today.

   a. again   **b.** award   **c.** address

Many words have parts that come from other
languages. Use the root to help you figure out the
meanings of these words.

Root: *phon*   **Meaning:** sound   **Example:** tele<u>phon</u>e
from Greek

**B. Use the information about the Greek root *phon* to help
you write a sentence for the word below.**

4. microphone: _____

_____

 At Home: For each word that your child wrote, have him or
her identify whether the unstressed *a* is the first or second
syllable.

Name _____

In some words, the letter **k, g, w,** or **b** is silent.

Mary **k**nits. Her lam**b** **w**rites a si**g**n.

Write the word from the box that fits each clue. Then circle the silent letter in each word.

wreck	gnat	climb	knapsack
gnaw	write	knife	thumb

1. This is a kind of bug. _____

2. This body part is on your hand. _____

3. This is also called a backpack. _____

4. You do this with a pencil. _____

5. You do this on the monkey bars. _____

6. You use this to cut food. _____

7. This is another word for destroy. _____

8. This is another word for chew. _____

© Macmillan/McGraw-Hill

At Home: Have your child make up his or her own
sentences for three of the words in the box.

The Ugly Vegetables
Book 2.2/Unit 5

193

A. Write the word from the box to complete each sentence.

| scent | muscles | blooming | aroma | trade | prickly |

1. The flowers are _____ and ready to pick.

2. The _____ of fresh strawberries filled the air.

3. Are your _____ strong enough to lift this crate?

4. Let's make a _____ of my tuna fish for your peanut butter and jelly sandwich.

5. The _____ from the baking cookies drew us into the kitchen.

6. A cactus is very _____.

B. Write two sentences using two words from the box.

7. _____

8. _____

Name _____

As you read *The Ugly Vegetables*, fill in the
Sequence Chart.

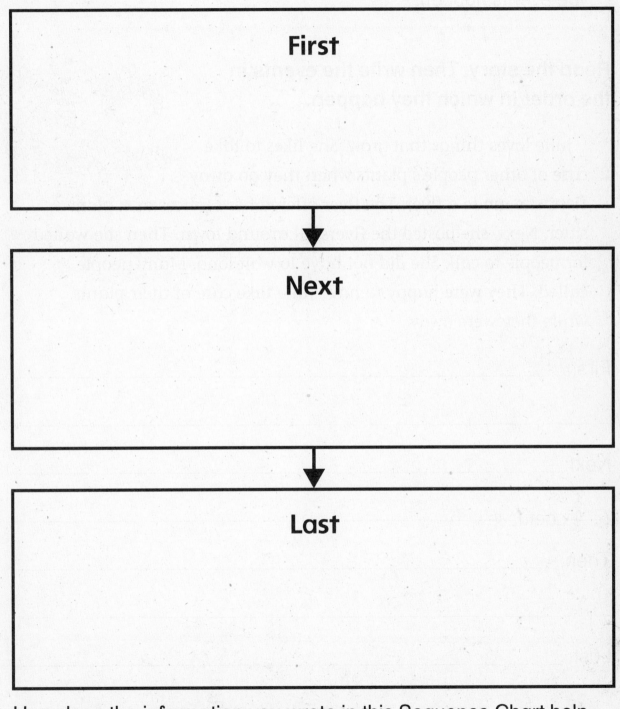

First

↓

Next

↓

Last

How does the information you wrote in this Sequence Chart help
you summarize *The Ugly Vegetables*?

At Home: Have your child use the chart to retell the story.

The Ugly Vegetables
Book 2.2/Unit 5

195

The **sequence** in a story or article is the order in which the events happen.

Read the story. Then write the events in the order in which they happen.

Julie loves things that grow. She likes to take care of other people's plants when they go away. First, she made a flyer. The flyer offered her services as a plant sitter. Next, she posted the flyers all around town. Then she waited for people to call. She did not have to wait long. Many people called. They were happy to have Julie take care of their plants while they were away.

First: _____

_____

Next: _____

_____

Then: _____

_____

Last: _____

_____

© Macmillan/McGraw-Hill

At Home: Ask your child to talk about how you take care of the plants at home. What do you do first? Next? Last?

Name _____

As I read, I will pay attention to the punctuation in each sentence.

10	Tomatoes are easy to grow, if there is enough water and a lot of sunlight. Tomatoes need warmth. Don't plant
20	tomatoes if the weather is cold and snowy.
28	Good tomatoes need good soil. You can grow tomatoes
37	in pots or in the ground. If the pot is big enough, you can
51	leave your tomato plant in it. If it is not big enough, you
64	will need to transplant the seedling into the ground.
73	As the seedling grows taller, it grows more leaves and
83	looks like a bush. People usually tie the slightly **prickly**
93	stem to a stake. The plant climbs up the stake as it grows.
106	Next, the plant grows flowers. This is the **blooming**
115	stage. After that, the flowers turn into fruit. You will have
126	to wait about six weeks before you have ripe fruit. 136

Comprehension Check

1. What steps should you take to grow tomatoes? **Sequence**

2. Why would you choose a large pot for a tomato seedling? **Problem and Solution**

	Words Read	–	Number of Errors	=	Words Correct Score
First Read		–		=	
Second Read		–		=	

At Home: Help your child read the passage, paying attention to the goal at the top of the page.

The Ugly Vegetables
Book 2.2/Unit 5

 197

Homophones are words that sound the same but have different spellings and meanings. **Wait** and **weight** are homophones.

They **wait** in line to go into the movies.

The baby's **weight** was 15 pounds.

Write a word from the box to complete each sentence. Use the other words in the sentence as clues.

know	no	wood	would	weak
week	write	right	tied	tide

1. Harry will _____ a list of all the presents he wants for his birthday.

2. Do you _____ if we turn left or _____?

3. Low _____ is the best time to find shells.

4. The flu made him too _____ to play baseball.

5. The fence is made of _____.

6. I _____ like to go to the beach next _____.

© Macmillan/McGraw-Hill

At Home: Have your child use the homophones *to, too,* and *two* in his or her own sentences.

Sometimes when two letters are together in a word, one letter is silent.

la**mb**　　**kn**its　　**wr**ites　　**gn**at

Write a word in the puzzle for each picture clue. The puzzle shows the silent letter in each word.

Across

2.

3.

Down

1.

3.

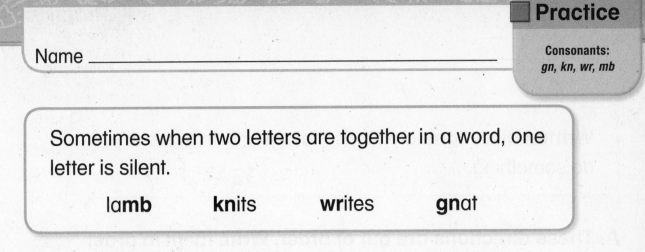

4.

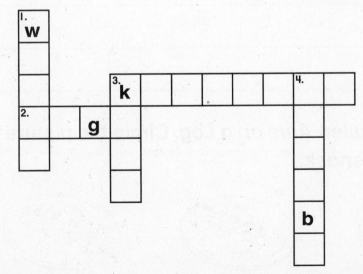

 At Home: Have your child use each word in the puzzle in a sentence.

The Ugly Vegetables
Book 2.2/Unit 5
 199

Written directions are steps that tell how to make or do something.

A. These directions are out of order. Write them in order on the lines below.

After filling the celery, sprinkle raisins on the cream cheese.

Wash and dry a stalk of celery.

Then gently press the raisins into the cheese.

Fill the hollow part of the celery with cream cheese.

I. _____

_____

2. _____

_____

3. _____

_____

4. _____

_____

B. This snack is called *Ants on a Log.* Circle the picture that shows the snack.

 At Home: Have your child write directions for a snack he or she knows how to make.

> The **c** in *cent* stands for the /**s**/ sound. This is the **soft c** sound.
>
> The **c** in *cap* stands for the /**k**/ sound. This is the **hard c** sound.
>
> The **g** in *gem* stands for the /**j**/ sound. This is the **soft g** sound.
>
> The **g** in *goose* stands for the /**g**/ sound. This is the **hard g** sound.

Choose a word from the box to complete each sentence.
Write it on the line. Then circle each word that you wrote
that has the soft c or soft g sound.

> car   garden   camp   sugar   circle   giant   face   huge

1. You have to plug in an electric _____.

2. Dad planted bushes in the _____.

3. The puppy grew into a _____ dog.

4. My baby brother can draw a _____ on the paper.

5. His dad seemed as big as a _____ to the little boy.

6. Jack's favorite part of _____ was boating.

7. My puppy uses his sad _____ to beg for treats.

8. Too much _____ is bad for your teeth.

At Home: Encourage your child to write six sentences using
any of the eight words in the box above.

The Moon • **Book 2.2/Unit 5**   **201**

Write each word under the correct heading. Then use each word in a sentence about the moon and the stars. Write it on the line.

spacecraft	footprint	surface
discovered	visible	lunar

Noun: person, place, or thing

1. _____

_____

2. _____

_____

3. _____

_____

Verb: shows action

4. _____

_____

Adjective: describes a noun

5. _____

_____

6. _____

_____

Name _____

As you read *The Moon*, fill in the Classify and Categorize Chart.

Observing	Visiting

How does the information you wrote in this Classify and Categorize Chart help you summarize *The Moon*?

© Macmillan/McGraw-Hill

At Home: Have your child use the chart to retell the story.

The Moon • **Book 2.2/Unit 5** 203

Name _____

> To **classify and categorize** means to sort things or
> ideas into groups. The items in each group are alike in
> some way.

**Read each sentence. Write the letter _M_ if it tells about
the moon. Write the letter _E_ if it tells about Earth.**

1. ___ The planet has water, so many plants and
   animals can live there.

2. ___ It is an empty place.

3. ___ Its surface has oceans and many land forms.

4. ___ It has no weather.

5. ___ It has no water so it cannot support life.

6. ___ It is full of life.

7. ___ Its water also creates weather.

8. ___ Its surface is marked with craters.

© Macmillan/McGraw-Hill

At Home: Help your child to use the sentences from the
page to write about the moon and Earth.

As I read, I will pay attention to the pronunciation of the vocabulary words and proper nouns, and to the tempo.

	Many **spacecraft** have visited the moon, and 12
8	astronauts have walked on the **lunar surface**. Neil
16	Armstrong and Edwin "Buzz" Aldrin were the first people
25	to walk on the moon. The most famous thing Armstrong
35	left behind was his **footprint**! There is no air, wind, or
46	rain on the moon, so the footprint is still **visible**. It is there
59	to be **discovered** by another astronaut.
65	Some astronauts are now living on the International
73	Space Station. The station is a huge research center. One
83	day it may also be a launching pad to new places in space.
96	Maybe one day you will become an astronaut or live on
107	a space station. Right now, very few people can be called
118	star sailors! 120

Comprehension Check

1. Who were the first people to walk on the moon? **Main Idea and Details**

2. Why is Neil Armstrong's footprint still visible on the moon? **Draw Conclusions**

	Words Read	−	Number of Errors	=	Words Correct Score
First Read		−		=	
Second Read		−		=	

© Macmillan/McGraw-Hill

At Home: Help your child read the passage, paying attention to the goal at the top of the page.

A **compound word** is a word made of two smaller words. The smaller words often give clues to the meaning of the compound word.

Match each word in the box to its meaning.

airmail	firewood	spaceship	goldfish
lightweight	sandpaper	snowstorm	footprint

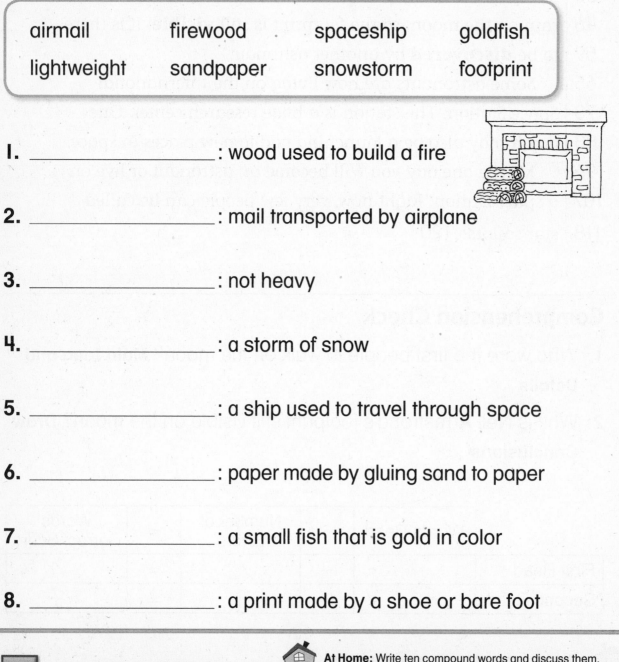

1. _____ : wood used to build a fire

2. _____ : mail transported by airplane

3. _____ : not heavy

4. _____ : a storm of snow

5. _____ : a ship used to travel through space

6. _____ : paper made by gluing sand to paper

7. _____ : a small fish that is gold in color

8. _____ : a print made by a shoe or bare foot

At Home: Write ten compound words and discuss them. Then decide together how the smaller words relate to the meaning of the whole word.

© Macmillan/McGraw-Hill

> **Soft *c*** stands for the /**s**/ sound. **Hard *c*** stands for the /**k**/ sound.
>
> **Soft *g*** stands for the /**j**/ sound. **Hard *g*** stands for the /**g**/ sound.

Circle the word in the box that has the same beginning sound as the two words above it. Then write it on the line.

1. good   games   _____

garden	gem

2. gelatin   germ   _____

gem	go

3. circus   circles   _____

could	cycle

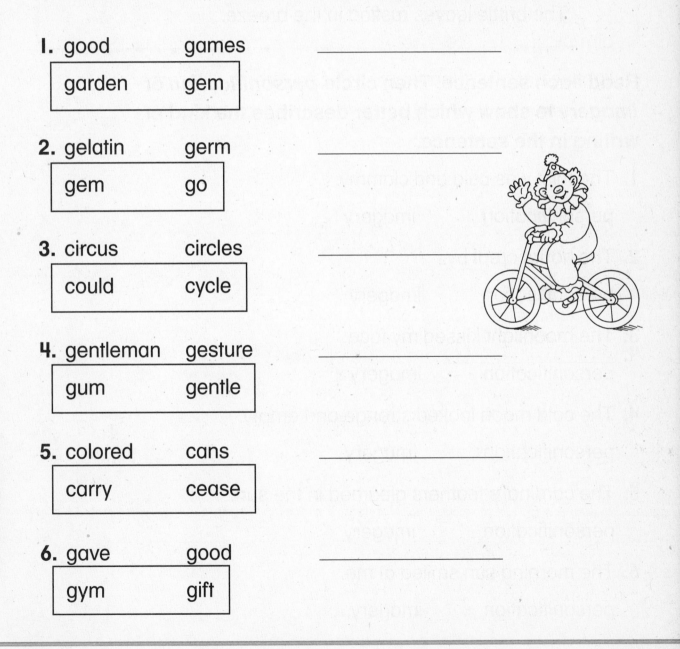

4. gentleman   gesture   _____

gum	gentle

5. colored   cans   _____

carry	cease

6. gave   good   _____

gym	gift

 At Home: Have your child make up a silly story using four or more words from this page that have a *hard* or *soft c* or *g* sound.

Name _____

Personification is a way of speaking about a thing or animal as if it were a person and could do things that people do.

    The door groaned.   The rising sun greeted us.

Imagery is the way a poet uses words to make a picture in the reader's mind.

    The brittle leaves rustled in the breeze.

Read each sentence. Then circle *personification* or *imagery* to show which better describes the kind of writing in the sentence.

1. The mist was cold and clammy.

   personification   imagery

2. The hours crept by.

   personification   imagery

3. The moonlight kissed my face.

   personification   imagery

4. The cold moon looked strange and empty.

   personification   imagery

5. The cardinal's feathers gleamed in the sun.

   personification   imagery

6. The morning sun smiled at me.

   personification   imagery.

At Home: Have your child find examples of personification and imagery in a book that you read together.

Use the words in the box to complete the story.

planet	voyage	beyond	joy	spacecraft
knew	out	around	surface	courage

I _____ space travel would be fun. I never

imagined that I would ever travel _____ Earth's

atmosphere. What a _____ it was to see the

_____ Earth from space. It was really exciting

when we landed the _____ on the moon's

_____. The commander asked me if I wanted

to get _____ of the spacecraft and walk. I said

yes. That took a lot of _____. My first space

_____ was out of this world!

Name _____

A. Match the definition to the word. Then write the letter of the word on the line.

1. a hole in the ground that an animal uses ___   a. scent

2. done without any plan ___   b. areas

3. an exchange ___   c. visible

4. a smell ___   d. burrow

5. body parts that make your body move ___   e. gathered

6. brought together ___   f. muscles

7. able to be seen ___   g. randomly

8. parts of a place ___   h. trade

B. Write two sentences that tell about the picture. Use the words *warning* and *signal*.

_____

_____

_____

The letters **-dge** and **-ge** stand for the sound /j/.

Choose a word from the box to complete each sentence. Write the word on the line. Then circle the letters that stand for the sound /j/ at the end of each word you wrote.

change	bulge	charge	range
cage	damage	fudge	large

1. The bird was in its _____.

2. The toy was too _____ to fit into the box.

3. My grandma makes delicious _____.

4. The storm caused _____ to the roof.

5. Charles wanted to _____ the television channel.

6. The shirts are available in a _____ of colors.

7. The library will _____ a late fee for overdue books.

8. The bag was so full that it started to _____.

At Home: Ask your child to name words that end with *nge, rge, dge, lge,* and *ge* and then use each word in a sentence.

Mice and Beans • Book 2.2/Unit 6   211

A. Choose the correct word from the box to match each definition below. Write the word on the line. Then number the words so they are in ABC order.

| fetch   simmered   menu   assembled   devoured   forgetting |

1. not remembering _____ ____

2. put together _____ ____

3. to go get _____ ____

4. cooked on low heat on a stove _____ ____

5. ate greedily _____ ____

6. foods being served _____ ____

B. Write two sentences using words from the box.

7. _____

_____

8. _____

_____

Name _____

**As you read *Mice and Beans*, fill in the
Reality and Fantasy Chart.**

REALITY	FANTASY
What Could Happen?	What Could Not Happen?

How does the information you wrote in this Reality and Fantasy
Chart help you to better understand *Mice and Beans*?

At Home: Have your child use the chart to retell the story.

© Macmillan/McGraw-Hill

Fantasy is something that cannot happen in real life.

Reality is something that can happen in real life.

Read each sentence. Write *reality* if it tells about something that could really happen. Write *fantasy* if it tells about something that could not really happen.

I. The chair walked across the street. _____

2. The birds flew across the sky. _____

3. Keith ate five hot dogs. _____

4. Lauren is starting school tomorrow. _____

5. The goat was shopping at the mall. _____

6. The fairy granted Megan three wishes. _____

7. The cat meowed. _____

8. The dragon flew over the castle. _____

9. Rainbows have many colors. _____

10. The giant lifted the house with one hand. _____

© Macmillan/McGraw-Hill

 At Home: Have your child write two sentences, one fantasy and one reality.

As I read, I will pay attention to expression.

	Roger woke up with the hot sun already smiling
9	down on him. He felt like it was going to be a
21	special day, but he wasn't sure why.
28	"It's the first day of summer!" said Dad.
36	That was it! Summer was here! It was Roger's
45	favorite time of the year. He thought about the
54	warm sun and the sweet fruits he ate each summer.
64	This year would be no different.
70	Roger and his dad always threw a party to
79	celebrate the new season. This year his dad made
88	the guest list. He said a surprise guest would be the
99	bright spot in the party.
104	Roger got dressed in a hurry. He was so excited to
115	bake with his dad for the party that he almost
125	knocked him over in the hallway. 131

Comprehension Check

1. What time of year is the story set in? **Character and Setting**

2. Why did Roger almost knock his dad over in the hallway? **Make Inferences**

	Words Read	–	Number of Errors	=	Words Correct Score
First Read		–		=	
Second Read		–		=	

 At Home: Help your child read the passage, paying attention to the goal at the top of the page.

Mice and Beans • Book 2.2/Unit 6   215

You can figure out the meaning of an **inflected verb** by putting together the meanings of its word parts.

Add the word ending to the verb.
Then write the new word in a sentence.

1. wear + ing _____

_____

2. celebrate + ed _____

_____

3. laugh + s _____

_____

4. confirm + ing _____

_____

5. giggle + s _____

_____

6. heal + ed _____

_____

© Macmillan/McGraw-Hill

At Home: Ask your child to make up three original sentences about a celebration that uses verbs ending in *-ed* or *-ing*.

Name _____

Sometimes words end with the letters **-nge**, **-rge**, or **-lge**. The ending sound /j/ is spelled **-ge** or **-dge**.

Read each word. Pay attention to the underlined ending of each word. Then circle the word next to it that has the same ending.

1. hu<u>ge</u>   judge   age

2. ple<u>dge</u>   ledge   strange

3. pa<u>ge</u>   stage   bag

4. ora<u>nge</u>   fudge   change

5. bu<u>lge</u>   indulge   garage

6. cha<u>rge</u>   range   large

7. ba<u>dge</u>   edge   egg

8. me<u>rge</u>   verge   smudge

 At Home: Ask your child to write a sentence for four of the words he or she circled above.

Mice and Beans • Book 2.2/Unit 6   217

> **Written directions** are steps that tell you how to make or do something.

Peanut Butter and Jelly Sandwich

Ingredients: 2 slices of bread; peanut butter; jelly

Directions

1. Spread the peanut butter on one slice of bread.

2. Spread the jelly on the other slice of bread.

3. Put the slices together so the peanut butter and jelly touch.

Write a recipe for something you can make.

_____

_____

_____

_____

_____

_____

© Macmillan/McGraw-Hill

At Home: Ask your child to look at a recipe and identify the ingredients and the instructions.

Name _____

The letters **ar** stand for the ending sound you hear in **car.**

The letters **are** stand for the ending sound you hear in **bare.**

The letters **air** stand for the ending sound you hear in **chair.**

Write the words from the box that have the same vowel sound and spelling as the name of the picture.

scar	stairs	flare	fair	pair	spare
glare	repair	care	cart	smart	afar

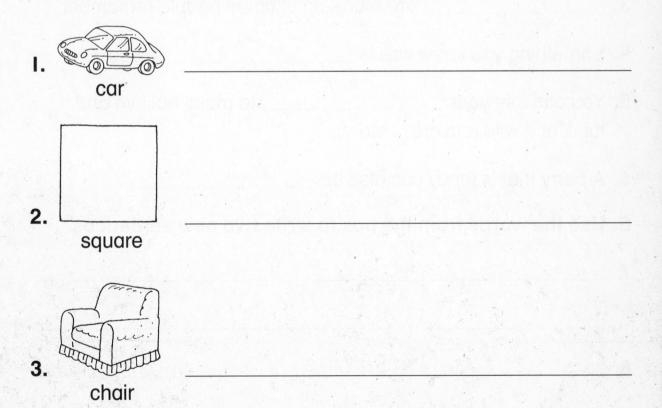

1. _____

car

2. _____

square

3. _____

chair

 At Home: Ask your child to write six words that have the same endings as the words above.

Stirring Up Memories
Book 2.2/Unit 6

219

© Macmillan/McGraw-Hill

A. Choose a word from the box to complete each sentence below. Then write the word on the line.

memories	imagination	familiar
glamorous	creating	occasions

1. People are _____ when they write books and draw pictures.

2. Birthdays and holidays are special _____ to celebrate.

3. _____ are made up of times people remember.

4. Something you know well is _____ to you.

5. You can use your _____ to make believe and think of a wild and crazy story.

6. A party that is fancy can also be _____.

B. Use the words from the box to write two new sentences.

7. _____

   _____

8. _____

   _____

Name _____

**As you read *Stirring Up Memories*, fill in the
Conclusion Chart.**

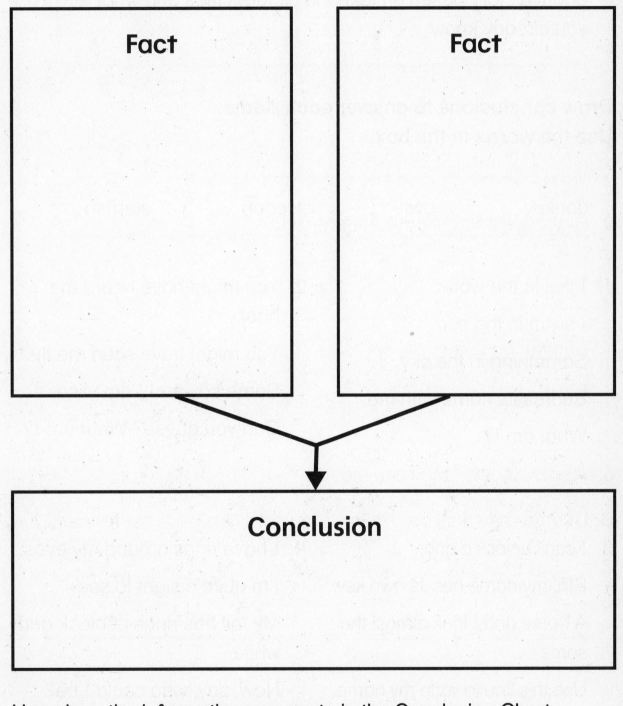

Fact

Fact

Conclusion

How does the information you wrote in the Conclusion Chart
help you summarize *Stirring Up Memories*?

At Home: Help your child use the chart to retell the story.

Stirring Up Memories
Book 2.2/Unit 6

221

When you **draw conclusions**, you make decisions about a story based on text and picture clues and what you already know.

**Draw conclusions to answer each riddle.
Use the words in the box.**

donkey	owl	raccoon	starfish

I. I live in the water.

I swim in the sea.

Something in the sky

Shares its name with me.

What am I?

_____

2. You might have heard me hoot.

You might have seen me fly.

Some say that I am wise.

Can you guess? What am I?

_____

3. I can't unlock a door.

Still, my name has its own key.

A horse and I look almost the same.

Use this line to write my name.

_____

4. I have rings around my eyes.

I'm quite a sight to see.

My tail has rings of black and white.

Now, say, who could I be?

_____

 At Home: Ask your child to draw a conclusion about what is happening outside if someone opened an umbrella just after stepping outside.

As I read, I will pay attention and copy tone and expression.

	People who can read are lucky. The world is full of words.
12	There are words in books and newspapers. There are
21	words on road signs and billboards. There are words on
31	maps and food labels. There are even words on television (TV)
42	and on your computer!
46	Words give us information. They can make us think. They
56	can make us laugh. They can make us cry.
65	Who puts these words together? Writers do. This book is
75	about different kinds of writers and how they use words.
85	Some writers write about the news. They write stories for
95	magazines, newspapers, the Internet, radio, and TV. They are
104	often "on the scene" for a news event. They **interview** people
115	there. Then they report the story as quickly as they can. 126

Comprehension Check

1. Do you think there are other writers than the ones who write the news? **Draw Conclusions**

2. Why do news writers have to report the news quickly? **Make Inferences**

	Words Read	–	Number of Errors	=	Words Correct Score
First Read		–		=	
Second Read		–		=	

At Home: Help your child read the passage, paying attention to the goal at the top of the page.

Name _____

You can sometimes tell the meaning of unfamiliar words
if you use what you know about word parts or word roots.
Some words in English have **Greek and Latin roots**.

**Read each root below. Circle that root in each word. Use
both words in a sentence.**

1. Root: **cycl**   The root **cycl** means **circle** or **ring**.

   bicycle   **cyclone**

   _____

   _____

2. Root: **act**   The root **act** means **do**.

   actor   **action**

   _____

   _____

3. Root: **graph**   The root **graph** means **write**.

   telegraph   **autograph**

   _____

   _____

At Home: Ask your child to tell you why *cycl* is a root
in the word *bicycle*.

Name _____

> The letter *r* after a vowel makes the vowel stand for a
> sound different from the usual short or long sound. You
> can hear the *ar* sound in *hard*. You can hear the *are*
> sound in *care*. You can hear the *air* sound in *fair*.

**Choose words from the box to finish the sentences in
the passage below. Write the words on the lines.
Use each word once.**

pair	stare	chair	apart	bark
garden	barn	stars	far	farm

I just heard my dog _____ outside again. I'm

trying to write a story for school. But all I do is _____

at the wall. Wait! Listening to my dog gives me a good idea. I'll write

about a dog on a _____. The dog goes for a walk

and gets lost. He is too _____ away from home. He

meets a _____ of birds. They teach him to look at

the _____ in the sky. That helps him find his way

back home to the red _____. He is happy to be

home. He likes the flowers in the _____. He likes

to sit on his favorite _____ in the house. He never

wants to be _____ from his people again.

At Home: Ask your child to write six new words that have
r-controlled vowels: -ar, -are, and -air.

Name _____

> **Word play** means using words or saying something in a fun
> and unique way. **Onomatopoeia** is the use of a word that
> sounds like the object or action it names.
>
>   The bees **buzz** from flower to flower.

**The words below have onomatopoeia. Use each in a
sentence.**

1. roar _____

_____

2. pop _____

_____

3. zip _____

_____

4. beep _____

_____

5. crunch _____

_____

6. splash _____

_____

© Macmillan/McGraw-Hill

At Home: Ask your child to tell you a fun sentence that
includes the words *crash* and *drip*.

Name _____

When the letter *r* follows a vowel, the vowel usually changes its sound. The vowel sound is no longer short or long. Listen to the vowel sounds as you say each word.

n**ea**r   d**ee**r   h**ere**   h**er**

Read each word. Then circle the word that rhymes with it. (Hint: The ending sounds that rhyme may *not* be spelled the same.)

1. hear

pair   where   dear

2. steer

clear   deer   care

3. stern

stare   fern   bear

4. ear

swear   peer   far

5. germ

term   wear   dear

6. jeer

gear   jar   dare

7. here

there   her   fear

8. nerve

deer   near   serve

© Macmillan/McGraw-Hill

 At Home: Ask your child to tell you a sentence for each word he or she circled.

A. Read each sentence. Choose a word from the box that has almost the same meaning as the underlined word or words. Then write the word on the line.

talent	treasures	impossible	pleasant	watch

1. Would you like to <u>look at</u> me while I play my drums?

    _____

2. Reading a long book in just a few minutes is <u>not possible</u>.

    _____

3. A warm breeze and sunny sky makes this an <u>enjoyable</u> day.

    _____

4. Your <u>amazing gift</u> for painting helped you to win the art contest.

    _____

5. A pirate would love to have this box of <u>very valuable things</u>.

    _____

B. Write a new sentence using two of the words from the box.

6. _____

    _____

Name _____

As you read *Music of the Stone Age*, fill in the Make Judgments Chart.

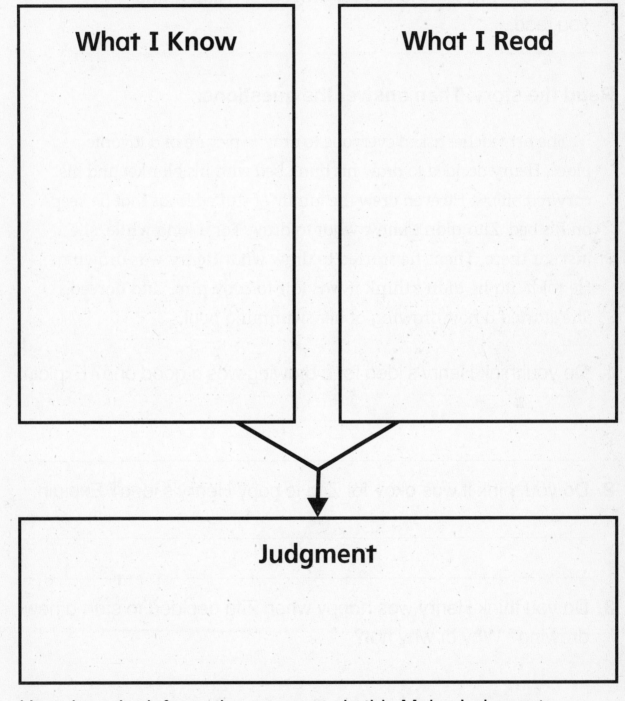

What I Know	What I Read

Judgment

How does the information you wrote in this Make Judgments Chart help you to better understand *Music of the Stone Age*?

 At Home: Have your child use the chart to retell the story.

To **make judgments,** you can use what you read and what you already know to form your own opinion about what you read.

Read the story. Then answer the questions.

The art teacher asked everyone to draw a picture of a favorite place. Henry decided to draw his bunk bed with his blanket and his cozy red pillow. He even drew the family of stuffed frogs that he keeps on his bed. Zita didn't know what to draw. For a long while, she just sat there. Then she started to draw what Henry was drawing. He told Zita he didn't think it was fair to copy him. Zita agreed. She started a new drawing of her swimming pool.

1. Do you think Henry's idea for a drawing was a good one? Explain.

_____

_____

2. Do you think it was okay for Zita to copy Henry's idea? Explain.

_____

_____

3. Do you think Henry was happy when Zita decided to start a new drawing? Why or why not?

_____

_____

© Macmillan/McGraw-Hill

 At Home: Reread the story with your child. Then discuss how Zita probably felt at different points in the story.

Name _____

> Some words can have more than one meaning. They are called **multiple-meaning words**. You can look at the other words in the sentence to help you decide which meaning fits best in the sentence.
>
> I hit the baseball with a **bat**.
>
> The **bat** flew out of the cave at night.

Read each sentence. Then write the meaning of the underlined word.

1. You can <u>lie</u> here to take a nap.

_____

2. I try to tell the truth and never <u>lie</u>.

_____

3. Cassie will start third grade next <u>fall</u>.

_____

4. Be careful not to slip and <u>fall</u> on the ice.

_____

5. I have a cast on my <u>right</u> arm.

_____

6. You chose the <u>right</u> answer.

_____

At Home: Challenge your child to think of more multiple-meaning words and give the meanings of each word.

Name _____

> **Dictionaries** and **encyclopedias** give different kinds of facts.

A. Write *dictionary* or *encyclopedia* to complete each description of a reference source.

1. A(n) _____ is a book or collection of books that gives detailed information about many different topics. Entries may include maps, charts, graphs, and photos.

2. A(n) _____ is a book that gives definitions of words, their pronunciations, parts of speech, and sometimes example sentences.

B. Which reference source would be better to help you find the following kinds of information?

3. What part of speech is the word ***style***? _____

4. Where and when did the art of origami begin?

_____

5. Who are some famous artists from Italy? _____

6. What does *piñata* mean? _____

At Home: Ask your child whether to use a dictionary or an encyclopedia to find out about Japanese art and how to pronounce the word *ballet*.

© Macmillan/McGraw-Hill

As I read, I will pay attention to the pronunciation of the vocabulary word.

	Cats have been around for thousands of years. Long ago,
10	cats were more than house pets. People thought that they
20	had special powers. Artists painted pictures of cats. They also
30	created sculptures of cats.
34	Today, we can see paintings and sculptures of cats in museums.
45	Thousands of years ago in ancient Egypt, cats were honored
55	animals. The Egyptians loved cats so much that one of their
66	gods had the head of a cat. People who hurt cats were punished.
79	Cats were thought of as **treasures**.
85	The ancient Romans also liked cats. They thought cats were a
96	symbol of being free.
100	The mosaic (*moh-ZAY-ik*) above was made hundreds of years
108	ago in Italy. A mosaic is made from small colored squares of stone,
121	glass, or tiles. The squares are put together to make a picture. 133

Comprehension Check

1. Why was hurting cats a crime in ancient Egypt? **Reread**

2. How was the ancient Romans' belief about cats different from the ancient Egyptians'? **Compare and Contrast**

	Words Read	–	Number of Errors	=	Words Correct Score
First Read		–		=	
Second Read		–		=	

At Home: Help your child read the passage, paying attention to the goal at the top of the page.

Name _____

Say each word. Listen to the sounds that the letters in dark type stand for.

tear   **pee**r   **ter**m   **here**

Write the word from the box that completes each sentence.

herd	deer	perch	here
germs	ears	hear	nerves

1. Did you _____ the song Joey wrote?

2. When did you move _____ from Ohio?

3. I like to help my grandfather _____ the cows.

4. This little bird can _____ on your finger.

5. My _____ were cold so I put on my hat.

6. The _____ in my body send messages to my brain.

7. I saw two _____ when I was hiking yesterday.

8. Cover your mouth when you cough to not spread

_____ .

© Macmillan/McGraw-Hill

At Home: Ask your child to suggest rhyming words for the words in the box.

The letters **or, ore,** and **oar** stand for the same sound.

p**or**t   b**oar**   m**ore**

A. Write a word from the box to complete each question.

| chores | oar | shore | storm | soar | thorns |

I. Do those roses have _____?

2. What _____ do you do to help out at home?

3. Have you ever watched eagles _____ overhead?

4. Is it cooler by the _____ in the summer?

5. Does the rowboat have a spare _____?

6. How long do you think the _____ will last?

B. Use two words from the box in new sentences. Write the sentences on the lines.

7. _____

8. _____

© Macmillan/McGraw-Hill

At Home: Have your child say and write five words that rhyme with the words in the box.

African-American Inventors
Book 2.2/Unit 6   235

Name _____

A. Write a word from the box to complete each sentence.

powerful	allowed	products
design	instrument	invented

I. The city _____ thousands of people to gather in the park for a concert.

2. The new medical _____ helped the doctors find the problem.

3. The _____ beam of light could be seen for miles.

4. Many new _____ are for sale every year.

5. The _____ for the new building was unlike any other building's in town.

6. My hero is the person who _____ peanut butter!

B. Write two sentences that each use one word from the box.

7. _____

8. _____

Name _____

As you read *African-American Inventors,* fill in the
Compare and Contrast Chart.

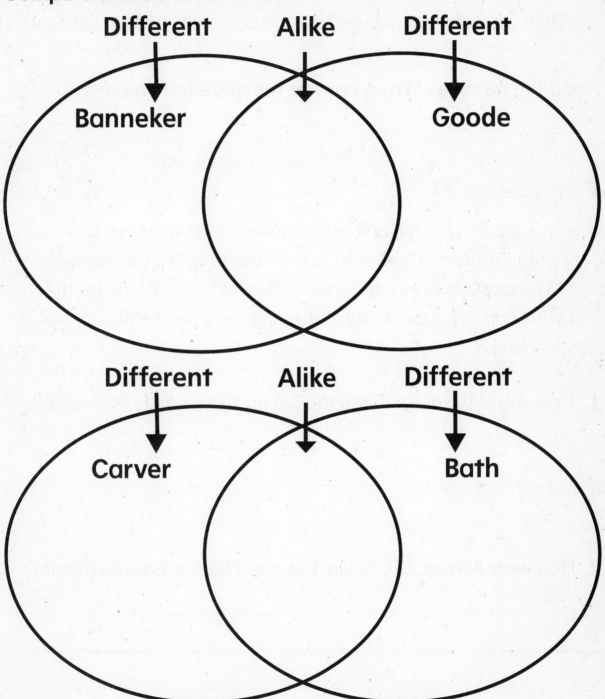

Different   Alike   Different

Banneker   Goode

Different   Alike   Different

Carver   Bath

How does the information you wrote in this Compare and Contrast
Chart help you to better understand *African-American Inventors?*

 **At Home:** Have your child use the chart to retell the story.

When you **compare,** you tell how two or more things are alike.

When you **contrast,** you tell how two or more things are different.

Read the passage. Then answer the questions below.

Alexander Graham Bell was an inventor. He was born in Scotland in 1849. Alexander Graham Bell invented the telephone.

Thomas Edison was an inventor. He was born in America in 1849. Thomas Edison invented the light bulb, movie camera, and phonograph.

1. How were Alexander Graham Bell and Thomas Edison alike?

_____

_____

_____

2. How were Alexander Graham Bell and Thomas Edison different?

_____

_____

_____

_____

_____

 At Home: Ask your child to compare and contrast two household appliances, such as a microwave and a toaster.

As I read, I will pay attention to the pronunciation of the vocabulary words.

9	In the 1880s, Karl Benz and Gottlieb Daimler built the first cars that used gasoline. These looked more like the cars
20	we drive today. So, in a way, Benz and Daimler were the first
33	to **invent** modern cars.
37	The first cars cost too much for most people to buy. Henry Ford
50	was an American car maker. He started making cars on an
61	assembly line. On an assembly line each worker does only one
72	job. This is a much faster, cheaper way of making things. Today,
84	many cars and other **products** are made this way in factories.
95	Before assembly lines, it took Ford's workers more than
104	12 hours to make one car. After, it took only 90 minutes.
114	By the 1920s, Ford was making one car every 43 seconds!
123	Because they were cheap to make, Ford's cars were cheap
133	to buy. This **allowed** more people to own a car. 143

Comprehension Check

1. How were cars different after Ford's assembly line? **Compare and Contrast**

2. Do you think the assembly line changed businesses other than auto making? **Draw Conclusions**

	Words Read	−	Number of Errors	=	Words Correct Score
First Read		−		=	
Second Read		−		=	

© Macmillan/McGraw-Hill

 At Home: Help your child read the passage, paying attention to the goal at the top of the page.

African-American Inventors
Book 2.2/Unit 6

239

A **suffix** is a word part added to the end of a base word.
It changes the meaning of the base word.

**A. Add –*ful* and –*less* to each word. Then write what
each new word means.**

1. cheer _____ _____

2. cheer _____ _____

3. harm _____ _____

4. harm _____ _____

5. care _____ _____

6. care _____ _____

7. power _____ _____

8. power _____ _____

**B. Pick two words you wrote above. Then use each word
in a sentence.**

9. _____

10. _____

© Macmillan/McGraw-Hill

At Home: Have your child make sentences for the other
words he or she wrote.

Name _____

Many words with the same base word have meanings
that are related.

The related words **sign** and **signal** both have to do with
acts or symbols that send messages.

**A. Match the related words to their meanings. Write the
letter of the meaning on the line.**

1. aboard _____   **a.** to get back on a vehicle

2. boarding _____   **b.** being on a vehicle

3. reboard _____   **c.** getting on a vehicle

B. Write the related word that completes each sentence.

unmarked   remarkable   marking   marker

4. She used a yellow _____ to highlight the
   important ideas in the story.

5. The police who were in an _____ car in front of
   the bank caught the bank robber.

6. Everyone was talking about that _____ piece of art.

 At Home: Help your child look for related words in a
magazine or book. Then write the words and let your child
circle the base words.

Name _____

A **time line** shows when important things happened.

Use the time line to answer the questions.

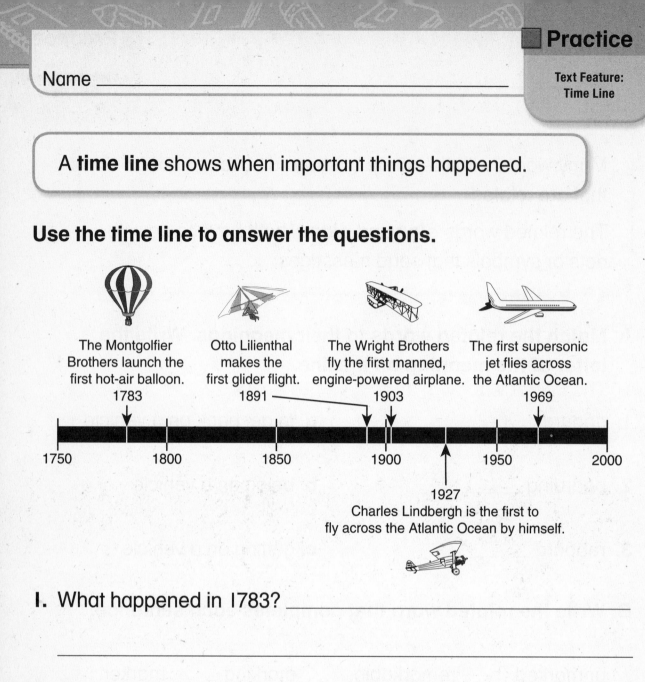

The Montgolfier Brothers launch the first hot-air balloon. 1783

Otto Lilienthal makes the first glider flight. 1891

The Wright Brothers fly the first manned, engine-powered airplane. 1903

The first supersonic jet flies across the Atlantic Ocean. 1969

1750　　1800　　1850　　1900　　1950　　2000

1927
Charles Lindbergh is the first to fly across the Atlantic Ocean by himself.

1. What happened in 1783? _____

_____

2. When did Lindbergh cross the Atlantic Ocean? _____

3. What happened 24 years before Lindbergh's flight? _____

_____

_____

4. How many years after Lilienthal's glider flight did the Wright

Brothers fly? _____

 At Home: Help your child list other machines that fly. Then use the library or Internet to find out more about one of them.

© Macmillan/McGraw-Hill

Name _____

> The letters *ire* and *ier* stand for the sound you hear in
> *fire* and *drier*. The letters *ure* stand for the sound you
> hear in *lure*.

Fill in the bubble next to the word that has the same vowel sound as the underlined word in each sentence.

1. The doctor worked hard to <u>cure</u> her illness.

   ○ cut   ○ pure   ○ cone

2. He will <u>hire</u> me to rake his leaves.

   ○ drier   ○ here   ○ wear

3. Are you <u>sure</u> this is the way to the zoo?

   ○ secure   ○ fur   ○ stir

4. We will <u>lure</u> the wolf into the cage and then move it to safety.

   ○ learn   ○ mature   ○ lurk

5. If you are cold, go sit by the <u>fire</u>.

   ○ ice   ○ fur   ○ flier

6. Let's help the woman change her flat <u>tire</u>.

   ○ tried   ○ wire   ○ turn

At Home: Say *-ure, -ier,* or *-ire* words and have your child
think of a word that rhymes with each one.

Babu's Song • **Book 2.2/Unit 6** **243**

Name _____

A. Choose the word from the box that best completes the sentence. Write it on the line.

goalie   figure   vendors   concern   collection   exclaimed

1. My _____ for the picnic is that it may rain.

2. "What a beautiful rainbow!" Kate _____.

3. The _____ caught the ball and saved the game.

4. The craft _____ set up their goods on tables on the sidewalk.

5. I can carve an animal _____ out of wood.

6. I have a _____ of dolls from all over the world.

B. Write two sentences using as many words from the box as you can.

7. _____

_____

8. _____

_____

Name _____

As you read *Babu's Song*, fill in the Character and Setting Chart.

Characters	Setting

How does the information you wrote in this Character and Setting Chart help you to better understand *Babu's Song*?

At Home: Have your child use the chart to retell the story.

Name _____

> Analyzing the **setting** helps you understand how the place and time affect what the characters do and say.

Read the story. Then circle the best answer to each question.

It was so hot! Even though it was early morning, Trista's clothes were already too heavy for the heat. Trista pushed through the door of the small clothing shop. The woman behind the counter smiled at her and asked her something in a language Trista could not understand. Trista pointed to one of the cool cotton outfits and pointed to herself hopefully. The woman smiled, looked through a rack of clothing, and pulled out an outfit that was just her size. Ten minutes later Trista was back in the street, cooler, and happier.

1. Trista is a: ___

   a. woman

   b. wild animal

   c. young boy

2. Trista probably: ___

   a. visits this place all the time

   b. does not like this place

   c. has not visited this place often

3. She seems to be in: ___

   a. her home town

   b. a foreign country

   c. a zoo

4. This story takes place: ___

   a. in a place that is very hot

   b. in a place that is cold

   c. in a forest

© Macmillan/McGraw-Hill

At Home: As you read together, have your child tell you what he or she has learned about the characters and setting of this story so far.

As I read, I will pay attention to the punctuation in each sentence and the tempo.

	Soccer wasn't just a game to Carlos. It was his whole life.
12	His father worked among the **vendors** at the local soccer
22	ground. He owned a little stall that sold meat empanadas and
33	fresh fruit juices. Carlos went along with him every Saturday
43	to watch the village team play.
49	Carlos and his friends practiced before and after school
58	every day. On the weekends they played games against
67	neighboring villages.
69	Their team was called the Mighty Lions. But they hadn't
79	been too mighty lately. In fact, they had lost every game
90	so far this season.
94	Paulo was the best player on their team. He dreamed of
105	being a Brazilian soccer star, like Pelé and Ronaldo.
114	"I'm going to score 1,000 goals," he said. "And help Brazil
124	add another three World Cups to its **collection**!" 132

Comprehension Check

1. How have the Mighty Lions done so far this season? **Character and Setting**

2. Was Paulo a great soccer champion like Pelé and Ronaldo? **Character and Setting**

	Words Read	–	Number of Errors	=	Words Correct Score
First Read		–		=	
Second Read		–		=	

 At Home: Help your child read the passage, paying attention to the goal at the top of the page.

To figure out the meaning of a word, look at how it is used in the sentence. Use **context clues** in the surrounding sentences to help you figure out the meaning.

Use words from the box to make the story make sense. You will not use all the words.

grandfather	grew	mother	Korea
friends	plane	boat	Texas

Today my _____ came to visit. He lives in

Korea. Korea is where my father _____ up. You

can still hear his old language in his accent when he speaks

his new language, English. My _____ grew up in

_____. You can hear that when she speaks, too.

My grandfather wants my mother and me to see

_____. My grandfather will stay here for two

weeks. He will see my school, meet my _____,

and watch me play soccer in the afternoons. Then my whole

family will get on a _____ and fly to Korea.

There, we will see where my father went to school and meet

some of his old friends.

© Macmillan/McGraw-Hill

At Home: Encourage your child to notice the text around unfamiliar words. Then discuss what clues the text offers about the meaning of the unfamiliar word.

Name _____

> An *r*-controlled vowel is heard in the *-ire* word family:
> wire, fire, spire.
>
> An *r*-controlled vowel is also heard in the *-ure* family:
> sure, pure, lure.

A. Match each word in the box to the set of its related words. Then write the word on the line.

> lure   sure   wire   tire

1. surely, sureness, assure _____

2. tireless, tired, retire _____

3. lured, luring, alluring _____

4. wired, wiring, wirework _____

B. Use a word from each group of related words in a sentence. Write the sentences on the lines.

5. _____

6. _____

7. _____

8. _____

 At Home: Look through a book or children's magazine and
have your child find *-ire*, *-ier*, and *-ure* words.

Babu's Song • Book 2.2/Unit 6   **249**

© Macmillan/McGraw-Hill

Name _____

A **map** is a drawing. It shows where places are.

Read the map. Then follow the directions or circle the best answer for each question.

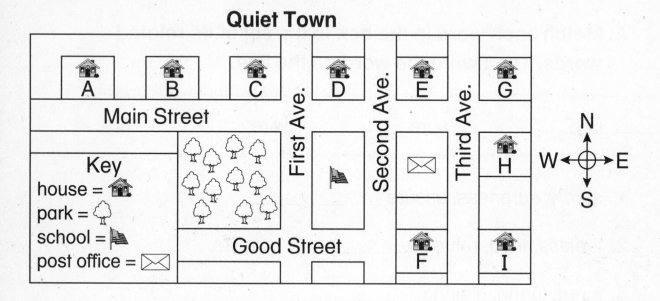

Quiet Town

1. Color the key yellow.

2. Color the school blue.

3. Color the post office red.

4. What place is shown on this map?

   a. New York City   **b.** Quiet Town   **c.** a state park

5. What kind of building does ⊠ represent?

   a. post office   **b.** school   **c.** store

6. If you lived in house A, how could you get to school?

   _____

At Home: Have your child look through an atlas and point out features of the map, such as color differences between land and water.

Name _____

Use the words in the box to complete the sentences.

| fetch | wedge | imagination | talent | powerful |
| design | figure | exclaimed | board | goalie |

1. I write on the _____ with chalk.

2. Use your _____ when you play make-believe.

3. The huge truck must have a very _____ motor.

4. Simon _____ when he won the contest.

5. My dog likes to _____ a stick or a ball.

6. My sister has a _____ for dancing.

7. The _____ keeps the other team from scoring.

8. Mom put a _____ of cheese on the plate.

9. The sculpture included the _____ of a cat.

10. Lu made a beautiful _____ for his picture frame.

© Macmillan/McGraw-Hill

Name _____

A. Match each definition to the correct word. Then write the letter next to the definition on the line.

1. allowed _____

2. glamorous _____

3. treasures _____

4. assembled _____

5. occasions _____

6. simmered _____

a. cooked at or just below boiling point

b. gathered together

c. let someone do something

d. special events

e. things of value

f. exciting and charming

B. Use the words in the box to complete the puzzle.

| dear | tire | hair | watch |

Across

3. Rubber wheel

4. This grows on your head

Down

1. Look or see

2. Sounds just like *deer*